Discovering
STATELY HOMES

Amoret and Christopher Scott

Shire Publications Ltd.

CONTENTS

Front cover: Wimpole Hall, Cambridgeshire. (Photograph by Cadbury Lamb.)

ACKNOWLEDGEMENTS

Photographs are acknowledged as follows: Sir Harold Wernher, plate 1; British Tourist Authority, plates 2, 4, 5, 6, 10, 12, 13, 15, 16, 17, 18, 20, 21, 22; A. F. Kersting, plate 3; The Department of the Environment, plates 7, 8, 11; Cadbury Lamb, plates 9, 25; The Trustees of the Goodwood Estate, plate 14; Christopher Scott, plates 23, 24, 26.

Printed in Great Britain by C. I. Thomas & Sons (Haverfordwest) Ltd, Press Buildings, Merlins Bridge, Haverfordwest, Dyfed SA61 1XF.

THE STATELY HOMES OF BRITAIN

It is not generally realised, even by people in what can now fairly be called 'the industry', what an incredible wealth of houses—I use the word in its widest sense—there is in Britain for the public to enjoy in return for the payment of a trifling sum. There is nothing even remotely like it anywhere else in the world. France, with its much longer tradition of gracious living than ours, has the *châteaux*, concentrated mainly in the south-west corner of the country, but many of them are crumbling in a most pathetic way, and stand unfurnished and unloved. The French have somehow never been oriented, as the British have, towards an intense interest in how the other half lives; perhaps it is something to do with Britain having a long-established and stable monarchy, with all that flows from it, as against the well-known pattern of history in France. But even this does not explain everything—Holland and Denmark have had long-standing stable monarchies too, but they are no more oriented towards the stately homes business than is France.

Americans, who would certainly like to join the league and would make a grand success of it if they could, simply have not got the basic necessities with which to do it; the oldest permanent building in the United States only goes back to the early seventeenth century. They have made excellent use of what they have got, and colonial Williamsburg (a restored early eighteenth-century provincial capital), for example, is a model of its kind. More recently they have revived some of the ghost towns of the old Wild West that have stood derelict for nearly a hundred years.

This is not intended to be a comprehensive description of all the stately homes in the British Isles. It is rather a personal choice from the several hundreds that one can visit, and it includes only houses which are open to the public. Short biographical details of some of the most important figures in the architectural and artistic world who were responsible for what the visitor sees today are incorporated; and a little space is given, as part of the general story, to a few particular features of stately homes which give them their character—plasterwork and staircases for example.

Throughout this book the phrase 'stately home' has been used. It should be added that the owners of stately homes on the whole hate this description; they much prefer 'houses open to the public'. Nonetheless, everybody knows what 'stately homes' are and for that reason alone this description will be used.

Some visitors will want to know what houses are available in a certain area, and will therefore be happy to skip from century to century as they go from one to another; others will want to concentrate on certain periods—Gothic, or early Georgian perhaps; still others may want to see different examples of a particular architect's or craftsman's work. All are catered for here, by listing cross-sections in different directions and by special mentions in the main text.

Times of opening and similar details are not given. Every potential visitor to stately homes should arm himself with *Historic Houses, Castles and Gardens Open to the Public*, which is published by British Leisure Publications, Windsor Court, East Grinstead House, East Grinstead, West Sussex RH19 1XA. It is revised annually and appears on the counters of most large booksellers in February. This excellent publication contains, in respect of nearly (but not quite) all the houses and castles that are open to the public, the essential details that any visitor is going to want to know — where it is, how to get there, what there is to see and to do, times of opening, prices of admission, and very often a photograph to give an idea of what the place looks like. Dealing as it does with over 1300 houses each year in a compass of 250 pages or so, the information has to be in précis form.

The National Trust

The largest owner of houses in England and Wales open to the public is the National Trust, a non-profit-making and non-Governmental (though it works very closely with the Treasury) charity; it owns over 200 historic buildings and gardens as well as 45 villages. It is fair to say that the enormous wealth of houses and their contents which the public can see in this country is very largely the result of the existence of the Trust. So far as the public is concerned the National Trust is an owner like any other owner, to whom one pays money in order to have the privilege of visiting his property. Since the Trust is an owner of hundreds of properties however, the public can buy the further benefit of what is in effect a season ticket to visit all the Trust's properties as many times as he likes in a year; there is in addition the chance of becoming a life member in return for a surprisingly modest subscription. Life members can visit all National Trust properties free (and take a guest too). The National Trust operates from 42 Queen Anne's Gate, London SW1. The parallel body which administers many stately homes in Scotland is the National Trust for Scotland, whose address is 5 Charlotte Square, Edinburgh EH2 4DU.

From the point of view of an owner, smitten perhaps by death duties and desperately searching round for some way of preserving the family home, the National Trust appears in the guise of a good fairy—though the gauzy wings carry a skin like an elephant's and a core of steel. The normal process is that an owner offers to the Treasury the house, with or without its contents, and with or without lands, instead of some or all of the cash which he would otherwise have to pay for death duties. If the Treasury accepts this, it will be on the advice of the National Trust which will normally administer the property. The Treasury and the Trust will require not only the house, but a sufficient endowment of land (as a rule) to make the whole bequest self-supporting. Within this broad framework, various minor bargains can be struck, such as the family being allowed to remain as tenants of the property for their lifetime. Certain conditions may be agreed with the National Trust about how the property is to be treated in the way of decorations, furnishings, alterations and so on.

At the end of the bargaining period, which may take several years, the owner is usually in the position of knowing that he has not got to find an enormous sum of money for death duties; and that the house will be preserved for his lifetime and for posterity. On the other hand, he has signed away for ever the family seat, together (as a rule) with a large amount of valuable land; the control of the house has passed into other, semi-official, hands; and the public, warts and all, has access to what was his private home. It is a hard, but eminently sensible, bargain, and it is this kind of level-headed bargaining which has resulted in the superb examples of architecture, artistry and craftsmanship that we find in such profusion throughout the British Isles.

The Historic Houses Association

This lively organisation represents the privately owned, lived-in houses. A modest annual subscription to Friends of the Historic Houses Association entitles the holder to free entrance to some 33 properties in Scotland, 7 in Wales and over 200 in England as well as specially arranged events for members only. Details are available from Historic Houses Association Friends, PO Box 21, Letchworth, Hertfordshire SG6 4ET.

English Heritage

English Heritage took over responsibility for many monuments looked after originally by the Department of the Environment or the Ministry of Works. Among the 350 properties in its care are a number of the country's most important castles, both ruined and inhabited, in addition to such historic sites as Stonehenge and Hadrian's Wall. There are Welsh and Scottish equivalents.

Season tickets, similar to those of the National Trust and the Historic Houses Association, can be purchased from English Heritage, Membership Department, PO Box 43, Ruislip, Middlesex HA4 0XW. Members receive an illustrated guidebook and location map.

It should not be thought that the habit and business of opening houses to the public in this country is a new one. It is certainly true that economic pressures and the enlightened attitude of recent governments and the semi-official National Trust has enormously accelerated the tempo of the business; but some families can point to a long tradition of not only allowing but encouraging members of the public to visit their homes.

In comparatively recent times, the great Duke of Wellington displayed in the porch of **Stratfield Saye House** during the 1830s a board, which still exists, saying as follows:

THOSE DESIROUS OF SEEING THE INTERIOR OF THE HOUSE ARE REQUESTED TO RING AT THE DOOR OF ENTRANCE AND TO EXPRESS THEIR DESIRE. IT IS WISHED THAT THE PRACTICE OF STOPPING ON THE PAVED WALK TO LOOK IN AT THE WINDOWS SHOULD BE DISCONTINUED.

The indefatigable Celia Fiennes was one of the keenest of bygone visitors to stately homes. Between 1685 and 1697 she travelled round England looking at many of the houses we visit today, nearly three hundred years later—among them **Penshurst Place, Forde Abbey** (she complained that she was not allowed inside), **Burghley House,** where she was somewhat put out by ' the immodesty of the pictures ' and **Chatsworth,** still in the process of being built at the time. This eyewitness account of many of the older houses in the country (*The Journeys of Celia Fiennes*, The Cresset Press, 1947) is another book to have in the stately home visitor's car.

We tend to accept, without thinking much about the reasons for it, the amazingly long time-scale of stately homes open to the public. There are several marvellous examples, wonderfully preserved and still lived in, of castles constructed during the Norman period up to nine hundred years ago. The main reason why Britain, uniquely, has this heritage is simply that through a combination of geographical position, national characteristics and a good deal of luck, we have not been invaded since William the Conqueror and his Norman knights landed near Hastings in 1066. Apart from such disasters as the Civil War, which destroyed or damaged a good many of the fine buildings in England, there has been little to interfere with the gracious aging of the beautiful houses that fill the British Isles. There are of course regional variations, some of them of great importance. The bickerings and skirmishes—and the occasional outright wars—along the borders between England and Wales gave birth to the type of great house which remains there. A factor on the credit side was the dissolution of the monasteries by Henry VIII in 1539, which had the effect (among others) of converting many ecclesiastical buildings into private homes.

Scotland, with its turbulent history, is a case apart: what went on north of the Tweed is reflected in its architecture and way of life. It should be remembered, by the way, that in Scotland the description 'palace' does not necessarily mean any sort of royal connection. It was a word used for the large domestic house, to distinguish it from the soaring and strictly defensive castles which were built largely in the fifteenth and sixteenth centuries. Another important difference between the stately homes of Scotland and their counterparts in England is that in earlier centuries good timber was very scarce in Scotland, and as a result much more stone was used in structural positions—and pine was mostly used instead of oak for panelling. Pine cannot be carved satisfactorily, and it was therefore very often painted in bright Scandinavian-like colours and patterns. Some splendid ceilings of this type survive, notably at **Crathes Castle**, Kincardineshire, and **Culross Palace** in Fife.

Anyone who spends much time visiting stately homes in the British Isles will soon become aware of the threads and bonds which run from house to house, linking this family to that by marriage, expediency or royal favour, by business or religion. The following of these threads is a fascinating pursuit and can develop, if one is not careful, into a lifetime's study.

HISTORY AND DEVELOPMENT

Many of the stately homes that are open to the public are important examples of the different periods of British architecture, and very often a house and its contents were created together as an overall concept. This chapter points out some of the particular features of different periods of architecture and decoration, and introduces some of the personalities concerned.

We can pass fairly quickly through the earliest periods of British architecture. There are no Roman houses left and virtually no Saxon ones (though **Chacombe Priory,** near Banbury, now largely Elizabethan, was lived in before the Conquest).

Norman (1066-1200)

The Norman period (also known as Romanesque) is generally accepted to have lasted from 1066 to 1200. Practically the only buildings which remain from this period are some churches and a very few castles. Norman architecture was characterised by its massiveness. Nothing was built very high, because with the methods used it would not have stayed up. Walls were built of rough-cut stone blocks, and relied for their strength on enormous thickness. Pillars were round, constructed again of enormous blocks of stone. Arches, and the tops of windows and doors, were always rounded until early in the twelfth century, when pointed arches were introduced. The decoration of the pillars that held up the roof was usually confined to the tops and bottoms, and the tops were far more important. The staircase in Norman buildings was always a spiral, each step being a single block of stone shaped so that the insides formed a continuous vertical shaft. Windows in castles were designed not so much to let in a lot of light as to keep out arrows and other missiles, and they are therefore tall and narrow. Internal furnishings were practically non-existent. The walls were bare stone; fires might be lit almost anywhere on the floor as there was no fireplace and no chimney of

8

any kind—the smoke eventually found its way out of the unglazed windows or the holes in the roof.

Although many houses of later date are constructed on the foundations of Norman ones, very few survive in anything like their original state. Examples of Norman houses and castles (usually the same thing) are: **Berkeley Castle,** Gloucestershire, still occupied by the Berkeley family as it has been for eight hundred years; **Rockingham Castle,** in Northamptonshire, built by William the Conqueror and added to in Elizabethan times; the lower part of the great Round Tower of **Windsor Castle;** and parts of **Tiverton Castle** in Devon, built in 1106.

Early English (1200-1300)

The next period, which lasted for a hundred years until 1300, is the Early English or Gothic. Here again we find that the surviving buildings are almost entirely churches and castles. In this period the churches became more important and the castles less so. Church building, particularly in the form of monasteries, was the main occupation of the age. A considerable number of these monasteries would not have survived as private houses to this day had it not been for the dissolution put into operation by Henry VIII. Examples of ecclesiastical buildings which were brought into private use in this way can be seen at **Forde Abbey** (plate 6) in Dorset (originally one of the most important monasteries of the West Country); at **Anglesey Abbey** near Cambridge (founded in 1236); at **Woburn Abbey** where the crypt (now housing fine exhibitions of silver and porcelain) has been preserved in almost its original state; and at **St Michael's Mount** off the Cornish coast.

The main difference between this period and Norman was that masons and builders had now mastered the art of construction in stone. Stones were accurately cut to be fitted together, and the result was that structures were much stronger for a given thickness of wall. Buildings therefore became higher and more graceful, and walls thinner, with the accent on height and related tall thin windows and pointed arches. Decorative carving on stonework becomes much more elaborate and three-dimensional. Characteristic of the more settled age, windows began to be used as architectural features and to lose their slot-like appearance; this was also helped by the introduction of window glass. Typical windows of the end of the period are, in effect, two or three of the original tall thin windows joined together under a single pointed arch, often pierced under the point with another circular window to fill in the bare stone triangle which would otherwise have been left.

The castle became a good deal more elaborate in its military appurtenances as well as its living accommodation towards the end of the Gothic century. Drawbridges and portcullises were invented, and castles were for the first time provided with separate living accommodation, still within an outer ring wall but divorced from the keep which had up to this time been both the house and the military headquarters.

One of the oldest and certainly the best preserved Gothic house in Great Britain is **Stokesay Castle,** near Craven Arms in Salop. Here are the pairs of vertical windows joined together under a pointed arch, and also here we see the beginning of the Great Hall layout which is mentioned further in the Decorated period which follows. In Kent is moated **Hever Castle,** home of Anne Boleyn. A smaller (and therefore rarer) house of the Gothic period is **Hellen's** in Hereford and Worcester; this manor-house shows one of the earliest uses of brickwork in the country.

Decorated (1300-1400)

The next age, from 1300 to 1400, is known architecturally as the Decorated period. This was a natural progression from the Early English period of the previous century, and it is the first one in which the large private house becomes of importance. Castles were still built; the chain of castles mainly along the Welsh coast, built by Edward I to keep the natives in order, includes **Harlech, Caernarvon** and **Conway** (all magnificent ruins under the control of the Department of the Environment) and **Chirk Castle** near Wrexham, privately owned and occupied until 1978 and little altered since 1310. **Lympne Castle** in Kent and, in the same county, the lakeside tower at **Scotney Castle** at Lamberhurst were built at much the same time.

We can for the first time see the comparative comforts of gracious living—admittedly on a fairly primitive plane still. The centrepiece of a house of this period was the hall; at one end was a raised platform where the lord sat with his guests, while the lesser members of the household and the servants ate in the main body of the hall at a lower level. Behind this dais was the solar, the private room for the lord and his family, often one floor above and approached by a staircase. At the opposite end of the hall behind a screen of carved timber were the kitchen areas and the buttery. Over the buttery was a guest room or a musicians' gallery—or sometimes both. The Baron's Hall at **Penshurst Place** has all these features in an excellent state of preservation.

The main architectural improvement during the Decorated period was the development of the window which now became a very important feature of churches and houses. Stained glass in particular became popular, and the pointed-arch style of windows (which was still the standard shape) was often filled in with elaborate stone tracery. The standard of craftsmanship in stone carving was extraordinary. This is far more noticeable in some great churches of the period, where work to the glory of God was pursued to the limits of the craftsmen's skill, than in domestic architecture.

Although houses with great halls were built, not many new castles were constructed during this century, simply because England at least had entered a period of peace and prosperity where (except in certain specific cases such as border disputes with Wales to the west and Scotland to the north) castles were no longer necessary as a way of life. A number of earlier castles were however rebuilt to give emphasis to the increasingly important idea of comfort in living at the expense of military might.

Perpendicular (1400-1500)

The next century, from 1400 to 1500, is the Perpendicular period. This is the period when several of the Oxford and Cambridge colleges (typically King's College at Cambridge) were built, and it was a period of welcome simplification from a style of building that was becoming over-elaborate and over-decorated. Important churches showed the characteristics of severe and simple vertical treatment in the stonework, enormous windows often filling the whole of one end of the building, and (representing the high point in solving the structural problem of supporting aisle roofs) fan vaulting. Domestically, castles were almost a thing of the past, largely because of the development and universal application of gunpowder. Castles were still built (one of the finest examples from this period is **Warwick Castle**) but their form was dictated more by tradition than by the necessity to defend them against enemies. Bare stone walls were starting to be covered with oak panelling as well as tapestries, and domestic windows, although nothing like the dominant feature of some of the magnificent churches of the period, were now big enough to let in a good deal of light. One of the particular features in the domestic architecture of this period is the hammerbeam roof, the finest example of which is at Westminster Hall in London.

The century proves a perfect example of the difficulty which architects and builders found in developing from one style to another—a difficulty which is still with us and always will be. During the fifteenth century a number of houses were built with battlements round the edges of the roof, battlements which clearly had no military significance whatsoever but were simply a hangover from earlier more turbulent days. Examples of houses from this period are **Oxburgh Hall,** Norfolk; **Alnwick Castle** in Northumberland (near enough to the restive Scottish border to be a castle in more than name), which is still substantially the same shape and size as it was when built; much of **Raby Castle** in Durham, a far-northern domestic fortress which claims origins with King Canute in the tenth century; the great hall, castellated porch and dovecot at **Athelhampton,** Dorset; and **Cotehele** in Cornwall, a grey granite mansion on a height by the river Tamar, with battlements against foes that were long dead even then.

Tudor (1485-1560)

With the end of the fifteenth century we also come to the end of the long period during which ecclesiastical building was by far the most important work in the country, and enter the new era where domestic architecture takes over. A great new influence is also at work—the Renaissance. This was the rediscovery, first of all in Italy, of the architectural and stylistic ideas of the Greeks and Romans. This is also the moment when we stop thinking about stylistic periods by the name of their characteristics (Gothic, Perpendicular and so on) and turn to the family that was occupying the throne of England at the time.

The first of these periods, then, is the Tudor period which lasted from 1485 to 1560. The Church, largely discredited by Henry VIII, took a back seat. Houses and palaces were built in great numbers, and we still have an excellent legacy of them. **Hampton Court Palace,** though later altered by Wren, dates from this period, and its Great Gate House survives practically unaltered from 1522. **Charlecote Park** in Warwickshire has another intact Tudor gatehouse. The most important change in domestic architecture was the widespread use for the first time of brick instead of stone. Bricks had first been used in East Anglia, and were imported from Holland. **Great Melford Hall** in Suffolk is an outstanding example of the great house built in Tudor brickwork. **Aston Hall** in Birmingham is a transitional house which in its architectural features looks back to Gothic and forward to Tudor.

Many great houses of the sixteenth century, in bricks of deep red colour that have weathered to a most delightful appearance, give evidence of how much the owners and the builders enjoyed themselves in the designing; spiral chimneys as if from a gingerbread house, elaborate carved painted and gilded coats of arms over the doorways, huge romantic gatehouses with mock towers and battlements, and everything covered inside with oak panelling, either plain or carved into the well-known linenfold pattern. The fireplace at last was a really important feature in the house, simply because people who could afford such houses were no longer willing to put up with the discomforts of icy draughts and smoke billowing about the roof—and also because the recent import for the first time of coal, with its far more noxious smoke and fumes, made it absolutely necessary to provide an escape. The fireplaces themselves, of brick or stone, were often elaborately carved above the arch opening. Examples of fine chimneypieces of the time can be seen at **Glamis Castle** in Angus; **Longleat,** Wiltshire; **Loseley House,** Surrey (plate 13), and **Sizergh Castle** in Cumbria. The bay window, introduced for the first time in the previous century, also became a feature of importance.

Not all houses, of course, were built of brick during Tudor times. There have always been regional variations in the type of building material used, such as the Cotswolds, with their golden Cotswold-stone houses and churches. In Sussex particularly, flint was much used as a weather-resistant walling material, and it gives a highly individual appearance to the few large houses where it was used in quantity; examples can be seen at **Glynde Place** near Lewes (a sixteenth-century house) and at **Goodwood House** (plate 14), one of James Wyatt's creations recently restored in magnificent style.

In some parts of England, timber was used for the main frame of the houses, sometimes in combination with brick and sometimes with plaster panels between the main timbers. The north Midlands with their huge forests were a particular area where timber buildings were the rule rather than the exception. Probably the best example of a Tudor half-timbered house is **Little Moreton Hall** in Cheshire. **Gawsworth Hall** (plate 24) in the same county is another of the highest quality. **Gainsborough Old Hall** in Lincolnshire is a fine example of regional Tudor building style using timber and brick panels. Stone was still used where it was felt to be necessary, and **Walmer Castle,** which is on the Kent coast near Deal, was a strictly military affair caused by an invasion scare (Henry VIII's actions against the Catholic Church were extremely unpopular on the Continent).

Elizabethan (1558-1603)

Queen Elizabeth I succeeded to the throne in 1558, and the Elizabethan period brought very definite evidence of the classical revival which came from the Italian Renaissance. Any imported style tends to get altered by the tastes of the importer, and few classical Greeks or Romans would have felt at home in an Elizabethan house. The way that classicism affected Elizabethan architects—and therefore their patrons— was a return to simplicity: straight lines, symmetrical shapes, carefully calculated proportions, strength and solidity. Typical of all this is the Elizabethan house shaped like a capital E, of which there are many examples in the country **(Doddington Hall** near Lincoln; **Hatfield House** in Hertfordshire; **Sudbury Hall,** Derbyshire, and **Parham Park,** Sussex). The E shape was made up of the great hall (a left-over from the Gothic period, but no longer used for the main living accommodation as it was then) with a long gallery above; at each end an identical projection at right angles to the main length, containing kitchens at one end and living rooms at the other; and in the middle (the short stroke of the E) an elaborate projecting entrance porch. The long gallery on the first floor was an essential feature of practically all great houses of the period, and gives a clear impression of the way of life of the Elizabethan gentleman and his lady. It was here that they spent most of their time, not in the great hall below. The hall was a showplace for the reception of guests and usually featured an enormous and imposing fireplace in stone, covered with carvings in a multitude of styles, and an impressive wooden staircase leading to the first floor, fashioned from two or three straight flights at right angles to each other, with elaborately carved newel posts at the corners. Particularly fine examples are at **Hatfield House** (plate 10), where the original dog gates, designed in 1610 to prevent dogs running upstairs into the main rooms, are still to be seen; and at **Blickling Hall** in Norfolk (by the same architect Robert Lyminge). The beautiful Painted Staircase at **Knole** near Sevenoaks, Kent, has survived in almost original condition from 1605.

The chimneys and windows of Elizabethan mansions particularly showed the new classical influence. Windows were absolutely rectangular, and divided symmetrically into a number of smaller windows by plain vertical and horizontal stone divisions (known as mullions and transoms respectively). Chimneys were severe and simple, and if they were decorated at all they tended to be disguised as classical columns, usually in groups of two or three or more.

After the widespread popularity of brick in the Tudor period, most large houses were once again being built in stone, partly because of its feeling of permanence, but more importantly because it fitted in better with the classical ideas that had taken hold of the artistic imagination of the country. **Burghley House** in Cambridgeshire is often described as the finest example of later Elizabethan architecture; this huge stone house shows all the features which have been mentioned. **Hardwick Hall** (plate 5) in Derbyshire is another typical Elizabethan great house, and it also contains an unmatched collection of contemporary furnishings.

So far as the internal ornament is concerned, the Elizabethan period—and to a lesser extent the Jacobean period which followed it—has no one style which can be called its own. It was a glorious mixture of the past, the present and glimpses of the future; Tudor panelling with Italian marble floors and plasterwork ceilings, strapwork everywhere, muddled up with all sorts of other decorative motifs—almost anything was acceptable. Decorative plasterwork for the beautification of rooms became important for the first time during the Elizabethan period. At first it was modelled closely on the vaulting of Gothic buildings, and only towards the end of the sixteenth century did the expression become freer and more naturalistic. Gothic plasterwork of about 1580 can be seen in the Great Hall at **Parham Park**, Sussex; formalised patterns of flattened ribs at **Broughton Castle** near Banbury, Oxfordshire; involved strapwork in the long gallery at **Blick-**

ling Hall, Norfolk (about 1625). The vaulted ceiling in the drawing room of **Glamis Castle** has fine plasterwork by Italian craftsmen who added the date of completion, 1621; and there is a huge naturalistic and coloured frieze twelve feet deep round the High Great Chamber of **Hardwick Hall,** Derbyshire.

It is this very uncertainty about what was right that contrasts so strongly with the succeeding era, when what would today be called 'personality cults' sprang up round a few architects who had given long and careful study to the principles of classical architecture, and who had then evolved their own styles based upon these principles.

Inigo Jones

The first of the new breed of architect, trained and inclined to put into effect the classical rules which had been rediscovered by the Italian architect Palladio, was Inigo Jones. He held from 1615 an official position as Surveyor General of the Works, and as a result some of his most important buildings are official ones: the **Queen's House** at Greenwich (part of the National Maritime Museum) is the best-known. No private house is definitely established to have been designed by him alone; however, he collaborated with a number of other architects, and one of the most celebrated examples of this is **Wilton House** (plate 18) in Wiltshire, with its famous Double Cube room. This, probably the best-known single room in Britain, is based upon the classical laws of strict proportion.

In spite of the rarity of actual examples designed by Inigo Jones, the English house from then on was vastly influenced by the concepts which he had brought back from Italy. The facade he designed was absolutely plain and regular; even the roof did not project above the walls of the house. The ground floor was merely an introduction: all the principal rooms were on the first floor.

Christopher Wren

Once again a new style took time to become established, and it also underwent considerable changes—often for practical reasons, because for example Italian houses were built to fit into a very much more docile climate than ours. The challenge of combining the traditional features of British design and the severe classical form introduced by Inigo Jones was solved very largely by another famous architect, Christopher Wren. He held the same job of Surveyor General to the Crown as had Inigo Jones. His reputation rests largely upon St Paul's Cathedral and the churches of London; this was to some extent an accident of history occasioned by the Great Fire of London which destroyed St Paul's and practically all the churches of the City of London in 1666, just before Wren was appointed to the position. None the less it was Wren who was mainly responsible for the design of house which we know as the Queen Anne style.

One of the principal features of the Queen Anne house, combining the classical and the traditional in a particularly happy compromise, is the hipped roof (the end wall no longer goes straight up to the top of the ridge). In order to keep to the strict laws of proportion which were the essentials of design, an extra floor was often introduced into the roof space, and the windows for this floor built out of the roof slope as dormer windows. Round the severely rectangular symmetrical sash windows were placed horizontal brick borders of alternate long and short bricks, with a flat brick arch and a wedge-shaped keystone above. The same treatment, using long and short blocks of stone, was very often used at the corners of the buildings. The door and doorway were of particular importance in the Queen Anne type of house. A common feature was a canopy, partly decorative and partly functional (to keep the rain off waiting visitors): one of the most pleasing types of canopy from this period is in the shape of a semi-circular shell supported on pillars and scroll brackets. Doors were almost invariably rectangular and panelled. Inside the house there tended to be a great deal of decorative plasterwork involving swags and garlands featuring life-like fruit, leaves, birds and animals. The whole effect was the very opposite of frivolity which crept in later, in the eighteenth century; the rooms were solemn, solid and dignified.

Grinling Gibbons and Antonio Verrio

Grinling Gibbons, probably the most talented woodcarver there has ever been, was employed by Charles II on his royal palaces, by Wren in the decoration of St Paul's Cathedral, and by many rich families who were building houses for themselves in the later part of the seventeenth century (Gibbons died in 1720). His best-known work in a private house is the Grinling Gibbons room at **Petworth House** in Sussex (plate 15) where the foliage, animals and birds appear to be alive on the walls; other fine examples are at **Belton House** in Lincolnshire (particularly the chapel); **Sudbury Hall** (the Drawing Room) in Derbyshire; **Lyme Park** in Cheshire and **Somerleyton Hall** in Suffolk (the Oak Parlour).

Towards the end of the seventeenth century a number of Italian painters and craftsmen were imported into Britain to help in the decoration of some of the large country houses which were being built. This began a tradition which lasted throughout the succeeding century. The best-known of the painters who worked in Britain before 1700 was Antonio Verrio, who was brought in by Charles II himself to help in the decoration of St George's Hall at **Windsor Castle.** Verrio then went to **Burghley House** where he spent twelve years, largely on his masterpiece, the Heaven Room. Other examples of his interior decorations can be seen at **Moor Park Mansion House** in Hertfordshire, at **Hampton Court Palace** and at **Chiswick House.**

The early eighteenth century

With the eighteenth century we are firmly centred in the age of the individual. So many fine houses were built, so many wonderful gardens and parks were laid out, and so many talented craftsmen, artists and decorators involved during the Georgian period that we must divide the many houses that one can see today according to who was involved in their creation, rather than according to how they fit into the architectural progression through the centuries. This was an age when many families became enormously wealthy, and were able to employ the best professional and technical advice to create surroundings for themselves which were not only a delight at the time and for future generations, but also perhaps just that much more splendid than their friends'. Architects, artists and craftsmen made fortunes if they could gain the reputation of being the only person that a man of taste would go to for a particular service or job: Paine, Wyatt, Vanbrugh among architects; 'Capability' Brown, Humphry Repton among landscape architects; Angelica Kauffmann and Antonio Zucchi among artists and decorators; Chippendale, Sheraton and Hepplewhite among craftsmen. All these went from site to site, from house to house, creating (with others of course) the masterpieces which have come down to us in such profusion, and which in many cases are preserved today in exactly the state in which their first proud owners saw them.

In the early years of the eighteenth century, for a brief but significant time, the Baroque style was all the rage. Nobody has ever successfully been able to describe exactly what the Baroque style is, but its effect on the beholder is overpowering. Ornamentation for its own sake was the keynote, based upon massive and dominating backgrounds. Two of the largest houses in England, both the design of Sir John Vanbrugh, are based on the Baroque style—**Blenheim Palace** in Oxfordshire and **Castle Howard** in Yorkshire (plate 21). Another huge house built by Vanbrugh (his last) is **Seaton Delaval Hall** in Northumberland. Castle Howard, magnificent though it is, looks as if it would be more at home in France or Austria. Alexander Pope was responsible for the following epitaph on Vanbrugh :

> ' Lie heavy on him, earth, for he
> Laid many heavy loads on thee.'

After Vanbrugh came William Kent, the most important architect of the second quarter of the eighteenth century. He was not only an architect but made himself responsible for complete interior decoration schemes as well. **Chiswick House** in London (plate 11) was actually designed by his friend and patron Lord Burlington, but Kent was responsible for the interiors. In this case he also laid out the garden, which together with the house was based upon the principles of Roman classical layout. Lord Burlington and William Kent collaborated again to design one of the most splendid houses in the eastern counties, **Holkham Hall** in Norfolk. This strange house, which reminds one somewhat from the outside of a Spanish prison, has probably the most magnificent entrance hall in Britain.

Robert Adam

William Kent and Lord Burlington were the last of the architects who modelled themselves severely on the principles of Palladio. The second half of the eighteenth century was dominated by Robert Adam. It was he who was responsible for the introduction of the classical motifs in decoration which rapidly became the rage; this was largely as the result of the discovery of Pompeii and Herculaneum in the middle of the eighteenth century. Robert and his brothers John, James and William, rapidly became extremely fashionable and extremely busy, and their work and influence is found throughout the country. Perhaps their two best-known houses are **Osterley Park** and **Syon House,** both on the outskirts of London. The proportions, the building, the decorative schemes and colours, even the furniture, were all created under their control. Both houses were, by the way, Tudor buildings before the Adam brothers set about them, and some of the original features can just be sensed behind the wealth of detail which the Adam brothers introduced as part of their concept—for example the long gallery at Syon, nearly 140 feet long but split by Adam into five bays. Another example of the Adam brothers' neo-classical work in London is the **Courtauld Institute.**

Robert Adam was a Scotsman, and some of his best work was done north of the border. **Culzean Castle** in Ayrshire is very largely his work; **Hopetoun House,** near Edinburgh, and **Mellerstain,** in Berwickshire, are both examples of Adam work through two generations, having been started by William Adam (Robert's father) and completed by his sons.

Among the foreign artists and craftsmen that played a considerable part in the creation of several eighteenth-century houses were Angelica Kauffmann and Antonio Zucchi; they not only worked together but eventually married (in 1781). Angelica Kauffmann was a Swiss who was brought to this country by Lady Wentworth, and who became a great success at Court and in society generally. She was originally a portrait painter, but later concentrated on interior decoration, working mostly in collaboration with Zucchi. She also did a numbers of commissions with the Adam brothers. Houses where work by Kauffmann and Zucchi can be seen are **Saltram House** in Devon, **Newby Hall** in Yorkshire and **Harewood House** near Leeds.

James Wyatt

Although the Adam brothers were clear leaders in the architectural field, there were of course many other architects working and designing country houses during the latter part of the Georgian period. Some of them, reaping the popularity of the new style which the Adam brothers had invented, produced houses and decorative schemes which are very largely copies of theirs. Among architects who were clearly influenced by Adam, but who nevertheless added a considerable part of themselves to the houses they designed and decorated, was

James Wyatt. One of Wyatt's masterpieces, the staircase hall at **Dodington House** in Avon, was based upon an earlier design by William Chambers, a well-known architect of the period immediately preceding Wyatt's; and this particular staircase design was then carried down another generation by Wyatt's nephew, Sir Jeffry Wyatville, in his work at **Longleat House** in Wiltshire. Another Wyatt, Samuel, was responsible for much work in the North of England. He largely remodelled **Shugborough Hall** in Staffordshire, and **Tatton Park** in Cheshire was begun by him and finished by his nephew Lewis Wyatt.

James Wyatt was much influenced by the first of the two Gothic revivals which had a considerable effect on all artistic forms. This first revival in the 1750s was typified by the Gothic novels of Horace Walpole and William Beckford, and it was these same literary giants who were largely responsible for the two houses which were the monuments to the style: **Strawberry Hill** and Fonthill Abbey. Sadly, almost nothing remains of Fonthill, which was Wyatt's great contribution to the new Gothic; and Strawberry Hill is not normally open to the public. Although a complete Gothic house did not appeal to many people, it was a popular form of architecture for libraries, where it was felt to be in sympathy with the spirit of learning. Particularly attractive libraries in the Gothic style can be seen at **Sherborne Castle,** Dorset, **Milton Manor,** Oxfordshire, and **Felbrigg Hall,** Norfolk. Both Milton Manor and **Audley End,** Essex, have Gothic chapels with their original furniture.

James Paine and Thomas Chippendale

It is one of the misfortunes of an architect—and this happened particularly during the eighteenth century—that his work can be radically altered by later architects according to the whims of fashion. Among early Georgian architects was James Paine, who was appointed to his first major commission at the age of nineteen by Sir Rowland Winn for the design of a new house at **Nostell Priory,** Yorkshire (plate 20). Paine left before the work was completed, and after a gap of some years Robert Adam was called in to finish the work, which he did of course in his own style.

This is perhaps the best moment to mention Thomas Chippendale, the master furniture-designer of the mid eighteenth century, for he was born near Nostell Priory and much of his best work is there. Visitors can see not only the furniture he made, but also many of the original accounts for these same pieces. There are other important collections of Chippendale furniture at **Wilton House**, Wiltshire; **Harewood House** and **Temple Newsam** in Yorkshire, **Stourhead** in Wiltshire (where there is a fine set of twenty-six dining chairs); **Uppark** in Sussex; **Burghley House** in Cambridgeshire and **Blair Castle** in Perthshire where there is an original account for 'a pair of large candlestands neatly carved and painted white . . . £7.7.0.'.

Apart from his work at Nostell Priory, the architect James Paine was also responsible for the stables at **Chatsworth** in Derbyshire; **Wardour Castle** at Tisbury in Wiltshire; and part of **Kedleston Hall** in Derbyshire, again virtually obliterated by Robert Adam at a later date.

Not only English architects were employed during the eighteenth century, an age when the arts of the Continent were of supreme importance in the British Isles. Among fashionable architects of the early Georgian period was Giacomo Leoni, who designed **Clandon Park** in Surrey and who was responsible for parts of **Moor Park** in Hertfordshire and **Lyme Park** in Cheshire.

The Regency period

The beginning of the nineteenth century brought what we know as the Regency style. There are few stately homes that are pure Regency. Most of the important architectural work of this period was devoted to public buildings and town houses, particularly in London and fashionable watering places such as Bath, Cheltenham, Tunbridge Wells, Leamington Spa and Harrogate.

The two leading figures of Regency architecture were Sir John Soane and John Nash. Soane was responsible for **Pitzhanger Manor,** which is now Ealing Public Library and may therefore be seen without difficulty (it was Soane's own country house), and for Nos. 12-14 Lincoln's Inn Fields, London, the Museum of Architectural Subjects; here is the epitome of Soane's thoughts and styles. Regency architecture was a most satisfying blend of the classic ideas of form, simplicity and pattern with individual additions—bow windows bulging out from a square front, and canopied balconies at first floor level are familiar examples.

John Nash would be described today as a town planner.

Regent Street in London (no longer as it was) was the centre-piece of much redevelopment carried out under his control. The **Royal Pavilion** at Brighton, built for the Prince Regent, is certainly one of his best-known works (though this extravaganza was not, of course, typical).

Arlington Court in Devon is one of the most pleasant examples of provincial Regency architecture in the country; it is the work of Thomas Lee, a Barnstaple architect. Lee also designed the great triangular column which is the Duke of Wellington's Monument on the Blackdown Hills in Somerset. **Normanby Hall,** near Scunthorpe, in Humberside, is another Regency mansion house (designed by Sir Robert Smirke, architect of the British Museum) which has been sensitively refurnished and redecorated in period style by Scunthorpe Corporation. **Leighton Hall,** near Carnforth, is a charming piece of Regency Gothic.

The Victorian period

Although one is tempted to say that the Victorian period was merely a rehashing, architecturally, of the styles of other periods, this is perhaps a little unfair; much the same criticism could be levelled at the architecture of the previous three hundred years. What was missing was any fundamentally new style. A number of stately homes (some built during that period, and others altered from houses of earlier periods) came into being. Among them is **Osborne House** on the Isle of Wight, Queen Victoria's favourite country home (plate 8). She, with the choice of Buckingham Palace, Windsor Castle and the Royal Pavilion at Brighton, needed somewhere quiet as a retreat and came here. Osborne is particularly interesting because it was designed very largely by Prince Albert himself, and his personality is stamped all over it. It is a sort of Italian villa, with tall flat-topped towers, like campaniles, and a balcony running along the whole of the first-floor front. It is a hotchpotch of styles, but itself created an Osborne House style that was followed by architects elsewhere in the country.

The second Gothic revival (we saw the first in the 1750s) was a mid-Victorian phenomenon. It swept through most forms of art, acquiring the status of a mania in some of them. One of the best examples of architecture in the Victorian Gothic revival form can be seen at **Knebworth House** in Hertfordshire. This basically Tudor mansion was completely Gothicised in 1843 under the influence of Sir Edward Bulwer-Lytton (the Lytton family have lived there since the house was built in 1540), another Victorian novelist. To modern eyes, the style (particularly inside) has little of the romanticism which ravished the Victorian senses, and presents an air of dark and brooding melancholy.

One of the greatest exponents of Victorian Gothic was Sir Charles Barry; his main work was the Houses of Parliament. An earlier experiment was **Toddington Manor** near Cheltenham, which has all the features (both inside and out) of the Palace of Westminster which followed. Another prophet of the style was Sir Jeffry Wyatville, whom we have already met in passing at Longleat. He was actually so immersed in the Gothic that when he was knighted after virtually re-modelling the whole of Windsor Castle in the new style during the 1820s, he changed his name from plain Mr Wyatt to the Gothic-sounding Sir Jeffry Wyatville.

There was a resurgence of castle-building in the Victorian era. **Belvoir Castle,** Leicestershire, the home of the Dukes of Rutland for some five hundred years, was almost entirely rebuilt in the Gothic manner during the early years of the nineteenth century, first under the influence of James Wyatt who died in 1813, and then inspired by the Duchess of the time who was a talented amateur architect herself. **Eastnor Castle,** near Ledbury in Hereford and Worcester, was built in 1814. It has all the features, and most of the furnishings, of a genuine castle of four hundred years earlier. Also of nineteenth-century vintage are two Welsh castles—**Penrhyn Castle** near Bangor, which was built in the 1830s for a slate magnate and shows it; and **Gwrych Castle** on the north coast near Rhyl.

A stately home which is pure and undiluted Victoriana is **Thoresby Hall** in Nottinghamshire. This spiky palace, with its deliberate riot of styles, offers examples both in architecture and contents of almost everything that had been thought of for the past five hundred years. **Holker Hall** in Cumbria, originally a house of about 1600, was largely destroyed by fire in 1871 and was then rebuilt in seventeenth-century style, with some unmistakably Victorian additions including a new wing. **Abbotsford,** Sir Walter Scott's house in Scotland, was built in 1811 round the small existing house; other major improvements were made in the 1850s. **Polesden Lacey,** near Dorking in Surrey, is a largely Regency house that was extensively altered in Edwardian times and now presents a rather Elizabethan aspect with its E-shaped plan.

Mention should be made here of **Ickworth,** Suffolk, an extraordinary amalgam of styles (plate 12); it is regarded as one of the architectural curiosities of the British Isles.

Its huge central rotunda is joined to two oblong wings (which are themselves different) by long curved corridors, the whole structure taking up a length of about 200 yards. As one might imagine, this house was the brainchild of one of the owners, and it took about thirty-five years to complete (1830). Another house which owes its existence and style very largely to the owner is **Waddesdon Manor** near Aylesbury, Buckinghamshire, which is in effect a French *château* on a vast scale, created by Baron de Rothschild in the 1880s.

An enormous house of the same period, also with strong French influences evident in the architecture, is the **Bowes Museum** at Barnard Castle, County Durham. Rather earlier, and certainly less flamboyant than either, is a pleasant house near High Wycombe, Buckinghamshire, **Hughenden Manor**, which was rebuilt by Benjamin Disraeli in about 1850. **Lanhydrock,** near Bodmin in Cornwall, is a large Victorian house based on the shell of a seventeenth-century one. The shape is largely Elizabethan, the battlements medieval and the contents almost entirely Victorian.

The Edwardian era produced more rebuilt stately homes of earlier periods. Among them are **Lotherton Hall** near Leeds and **Chartwell** in Kent, the latter filled with the personality and possessions of Sir Winston Churchill. More unexpected is **Lindisfarne Castle,** on Holy Island just off the coast of Northumberland. The castle, of sixteenth-century origins, was extensively altered in 1902 by Sir Edwin Lutyens, the major country-house architect of the time. **Manderston,** Berwick, however, is a rare example of an Edwardian house built regardless of cost on the grand scale of earlier centuries.

The urgent need to rescue examples of the crafts movement has been led by such groups as the Historic Housing Association, the Victorian Society and the William Morris Society. The result is that the public can now visit and enjoy, for example the Pre-Raphaelite period piece **Wightwick Manor,** West Midlands; **Standen,** West Sussex, one of Philip Webb's major designs and still furnished with the original Morris wallpaper and textiles; and the important Norman Shaw house **Cragside** in Northumberland. These are recent acquisitions by the National Trust, who have received them just in time to preserve their period unity in architecture, decoration and contents.

RUNNING A STATELY HOME

Why open to the public?

With very few exceptions indeed, stately homes are open to the public as a last alternative to demolition or sale. Let nobody get the idea that owners do it because they like it.

Private owners open their houses because they need the money to keep them up. Most of that money is not what you and I pay to visit the house but comes in the form of grants made by the Historic Buildings Council. The vital fact here is that, under normal circumstances, a grant for repairs will not be made unless the owner undertakes to allow the public access to the house. A good deal of investigation is made before any sort of grant is approved; 'Is the house worth it?' and 'Can the owner afford to do the repairs without a grant?' are two of the first questions that are asked in these cases. A grant having been approved, the question of just how the house is to be opened to the public remains to be answered. Some owners, particularly in the early days of grants, succeeded in getting approval for schemes of opening which effectively prevented all but the most determined of stately home visitors from ever getting through the front door. If you were to find out through enquiry that the only time you could see a particular house was on Thursday afternoons in March (and then only by giving a week's written notice to the owner of your intention) you would probably give up. This is a fictional example, but there are one or two houses in this country nominally open to the public but no easier to get to.

Most private owners have another factor to take into consideration. If they can demonstrate to their income tax inspector that the opening of the house to the public is a *bona fide* business, carried on with a view to the realisation of profits (however nebulous such profits may be), then all the expenses of opening the house will be chargeable for tax purposes against the income of the enterprise.

Problems to solve

The very first thing an owner has to decide (after his mind is made up that the house is to be opened to the public) is *what to show.* Is it to be the whole house or just one wing; or the ground floor only; or nothing but the gardens? Some houses like **Stokesay Castle** are important because of their architecture, and the interior is of secondary importance; others like **Waddesdon Manor** have outstanding collections of treasures. Some like **Penshurst Place** have a wonderfully preserved example of medieval living accommodation; others like **Chartwell** revolve round the figure of a famous occupant.

Very closely tied up with the 'what to show' decision is the vital question 'can the owner still live there?' With a huge house like **Blenheim Palace,** or even a comparatively large one like **Nostell Priory** the answer is probably yes. There will be enough to show to the public, and to make them feel that the visit has been worthwhile, even if part of the house is permanently closed to them. But what about the smaller houses where there may be only one room suitable as a living room for the family, or near enough to the kitchen to be used as a dining room? The owner may have to make one of several far-reaching, and probably very expensive, decisions. He may have to reduce the amount of the house he and his family live in to three or four rooms, and live in effect as a caretaker of the main part of the house. He may have to replan the layout of the house completely, perhaps making a new kitchen somewhere away from the main rooms. He may even have to move out altogether for the whole of the opening season, as in the case of **Stratfield Saye House,** and live in another house.

At the same time he will be considering the *circulation* in the house: the way the visitors will go round. Easiest in theory is ' in at the front door, out at the back door' but it seldom works that way. To start with, stately homes' back doors are usually the kitchen doors, well away from that part of the house where the visitor will be. And if you have a fine house that has stood unaltered for hundreds of years, you cannot start making new doorways in the facade to solve the problem. The result is usually that the front door is both the entrance and the exit, and this means that a circular route inside the house has to be planned and made very clear to the visitor. He must be asked to go *this* way, not that way. It can be done by arrows and signs, by one-way doors or gates, by helpful guides who tell you which way to go, by barriers (ropes or rails) which stop you going down the wrong corridor—or usually by a combination of two or more of these methods. The best method (or combination) is the one which works and which is least obtrusive. Anyone can put up fifty large signs saying NO ENTRY and fifty more saying THIS WAY; and this will certainly achieve a circulation. But the atmosphere of the house will be ruined, and the visitors will not come back.

Guides and security

Inside the house the owner must make a decision on *staffing* and the way in which visitors will receive the information they want. He can let the public go from room to room at their own pace, unguided and unshepherded (as, for example, at **Holker Hall)** or at the other extreme he can make them go round in parties under the control of a guide as at **Longleat.** He can choose one of the other methods which fall between these two extremes: there could be a guide stationed in every room to answer questions, as at **Felbrigg Hall.** There could be a recorded commentary to greet the visitor in the first room, and then occasional helpful guides along the way as at **Warwick Castle.** The visitor could hire a tape-recorded commentary which leads him from room to room and describes everything of interest, as at **Osborne House.** There could be labels on every piece of furniture and every painting, or there could be 'ping-pong bats' in each room on which are stuck sheets containing descriptions of the items of interest in that room (the system at **Stourhead).** There can even be appropriate music playing, as at **Burton Constable.**

The method of guiding (or lack of it) which an owner chooses is usually bound up with the problem of *security.* If one is inviting a hundred thousand visitors into one's home, with perhaps two thousand of them coming on one day, there is a fair chance that one or two of them might try to make off with something. Even more important, many people have a perfectly understandable desire to touch things, to feel the wonderful patina of a piece of Chippendale furniture or the lightness of a Sevres cup. This desire has to be restrained, and most people do it voluntarily. But where there is a lot of vulnerable material of this kind, then guides are necessary to see that everything is protected against damage and theft.

Maintenance is something which the visitor will rarely think about, but it can be a very considerable problem to the owner. For example, what sort of covering should he

put on the floors where his visitors walk? Carpets wear out
quickly, and if he likes carpets he may have to renew them
every season. It may be necessary to put down strips of
specially hard-wearing material along the main routes. On the
other hand he may want to show a valuable and beautiful
carpet and still allow visitors to walk over it; in this case he
will probably cover it with a transparent sheet. To give an
idea of the size of this problem, at Palace House, **Beaulieu,**
Lord Montagu had to deal promptly with the situation when
it was found that the inch-thick oak boards of the staircase
hall had been worn through almost to nothing by the feet
of up to half a million visitors a year. The problem is not
only an inside one; in America it has been discovered that
enough people walking about on the surrounding grass will
actually kill a large tree by packing the soil so tight that it
becomes like concrete.

The last important decision that the owner has to make is *the price
of admission*. Does the visitor pay once and for all, or are there to be
optional extras? Does he take one ticket which allows him
everywhere, or should there be tear-off portions for different
attractions. What should the price be anyway? The visitor must feel
at the end of his tour that he has had his money's worth, or he will
not come again and he will not recommend other people to come.

It is no easy task for an owner, even with the help of
experts, to steer his way to answer all these problems. Almost
inevitably he will make mistakes at first, and the results will
become evident—confusion at the entrance, the pork pies
running out at 1.15 on a Sunday, a hole appearing in the
carpet at the doorway to the State Bedroom, a bottleneck
at the souvenir stall, a vase missing in the Drawing Room.
He can only hope that his mistakes are not too important
and put them right as soon as he can.

GAZETTEER

In describing the main features of the houses which follow, I have not included any mention of opening times or seasons, availability of refreshments, price of admission or other similar details. All such information can be found in *Historic Houses, Castles and Gardens* published annually by British Leisure Publications.

The 200 stately homes described are my own selection from many hundreds. With a few exceptions, only occupied and furnished houses are included. They all have good furniture, pictures, china, silver and objects appropriate to their periods, and specific mention in any particular case means they are outstanding in this respect.

Properties belonging to the National Trust and the National Trust for Scotland are designated appropriately **(NT)** or **(NTS).**

Very many of the houses mentioned have gardens which are of great horticultural or historic interest. Space does not allow for specific mention of these, but they are marked with an asterisk*.

AVON

Claverton Manor, near Bath *

Home of the American Museum in Britain, and very well done with period rooms and American confections in the tea-room (which is disguised as a railway carriage). All this is hidden inside an 1820 stone house designed by Wyatville in true Regency style.

Clevedon Court (NT) *

Something of a mixture of architectural periods, but manages to retain the feeling throughout of a fourteenth-century manor-house, which is what it is. One complete wing was built in 1882 in the same style. The contents include a fine collection of Nailsea glass.

Dyrham Park, near Bristol (NT)

The present structure was built in about 1700 to designs of Talman. Handsome, regular and elegant, it contains not only a fine collection of pictures and furniture, but the most complete records (dated 1710) of the original contents of the house, many of which can be seen today.

Georgian House, Bristol

A supremely elegant example of Georgian town architecture. Built in 1789-91 and acquired in 1937 by Bristol Corporation which has with great care and sensitivity filled it with the best of contemporary furnishings, many of them local.

BEDFORDSHIRE

Luton Hoo, Luton (plate 1)

Although basically an Adam house, the interior is more remarkable than the architecture. Marvellous collections of pictures, Fabergé and Russian items.

Woburn Abbey

Scarcely needs an introduction, but don't be put off by the razzmatazz. As well as the Safari Park (with lions), the children's amusements, the Pets' Corner and the Antique Market, there are magnificent pictures, porcelain and furniture. Look particularly at the collections in the crypt (and their display techniques) and the model soldier display. On some days you can see the room full of Canalettos for a little extra.

BERKSHIRE

Littlecote, near Hungerford

Every king and queen of England except Charles I seems to have stayed here since Henry VIII visited on 18th August

1520, soon after it was completed. The interior is a mixture of architectural and decorative styles, though much of the Elizabethan flavour remains—particularly in the fine Long Gallery. There is a Haunted Bedroom and a Haunted Landing, apparently occupied by the shade of the same murdered child.

Windsor Castle, Windsor

England's largest castle (it covers 13 acres) and the largest inhabited castle in the world. Originally Norman but frequently altered and added to. State Apartments full of royal magnificence; but also a large collection of dolls with Queen Mary's own dolls' house.

BUCKINGHAMSHIRE

Ascott, Wing (NT)✻

Black-and-white seventeenth-century house with considerable additions in 1870s. One of the Rothschilds' family homes, with contents to match: especially oriental porcelain and Dutch pictures.

Claydon House, near Winslow (NT)

Dates from 1750s. The inside is quite remarkable—overwhelming Chinoiserie plasterwork and an inlaid staircase so beautiful that the visitor is allowed only to look at it. Many items of Florence Nightingale interest.

Cliveden, Maidenhead (NT)✻

The great terraces are all that remain of the first house built here on a magnificent site in the 1660s. A fire in 1795 and another in 1849 destroyed successive rebuildings, and the present house is largely the creation of Sir Charles Barry, architect of the Houses of Parliament, in 1850-51; further alterations were made by Lord Astor in the 1890s. Only part of the original sumptuous furnishings remains, but the great house, now a luxury hotel, retains the atmosphere left behind from the Edwardian era when it was almost the centre of English social life.

Hughenden Manor, High Wycombe (NT)

Disraeli's home for thirty-five years, impregnated with his personality and full of his possessions.

1. Luton Hoo, Bedfordshire, was originally completed c. 1830 but was substantially altered from 1903 to 1907.

2. Trerice Manor, Cornwall: the Elizabethan facade dates from 1571.

3. Wightwick Manor, West Midlands: the corner of the Great Parlour, showing the materials by William Morris and the frieze by C. E. Kempe.

4. Haddon Hall, Derbyshire, is regarded as the finest medieval house in the country.

5. Hardwick Hall, Derbyshire: the gallery of the Elizabethan mansion built for Bess of Hardwick, Countess of Shrewsbury.

6. Forde Abbey, Dorset: a twelfth-century Cistercian foundation which became a private house after the Dissolution.

7. Audley End House, Essex: the Saloon. James I described this house as too large for a king.

8. Osborne House, Isle of Wight: Queen Victoria's favourite country house, largely designed by Prince Albert.

9. Wimpole Hall, Cambridgeshire: a seventeenth-century house filled with fine furniture and paintings.

10. *Hatfield House, Hertfordshire: the Great Hall of the Jacobean home of the Marquess of Salisbury.*

11. Chiswick House, London: designed in the Palladian style by Lord Burlington and built between 1727 and 1730.

12. Ickworth, Suffolk: this extraordinary house was begun in 1795. The rotunda contains the main rooms.

13. *Loseley House, Surrey: the splendid sixteenth-century chimney-piece.*

14. *Goodwood House, West Sussex: James Wyatt's uncompleted design (1790-1800) built of the local flint.*

15. *Petworth House, West Sussex: the Grinling Gibbons room, decorated by the great wood-carver.*

16. Syon House, London: the Dining Room by Robert Adam is one of his most successful designs.

17. *Ragley Hall, Warwickshire: the Great Hall, with its magnificent plasterwork, was designed by James Gibbs (1750).*

18. Wilton House, Wiltshire: the famous Double Cube Room, the un-altered design of Inigo Jones.

19. Stratfield Saye House, near Reading. Home of the great Duke of Wellington (and still in the family).

20. Nostell Priory, West Yorkshire: the dining room, containing furniture designed by Thomas Chippendale.

21. *Castle Howard, North Yorkshire: this huge palace was built by Sir John Vanbrugh for Lord Carlisle between 1700 and 1726.*
22. *Plas Newydd, Clwyd, was bought in 1779 by two Irish bluestockings who filled it with the remarkable gifts of visitors.*

23. Leighton Hall, Carnforth, Lancashire, a Regency facade behind which is a unique collection of Gillow furniture.

24. Gawsworth Hall, near Macclesfield, is a fifteenth-century half-timbered house with a very rare tilting ground nearby.

25. Castle Drogo, Devon: a twentieth-century granite castle designed by Sir Edwin Lutyens.

26. Abbotsford House, Scotland: Sir Walter Scott's home, which remains as it was at his death in 1832.

Waddesdon Manor, near Aylesbury (NT)✲

Vast and astonishing French *château* (built 1880s). Another Rothschild house, filled with mainly French furniture, pictures and *objets d'art* of seventeenth and eighteenth centuries.

West Wycombe Park, West Wycombe (NT)

More than most, this house is the embodiment of the owner's personality. Sir Francis Dashwood had it extensively remodelled in the 1750s and 1760s as a place to entertain friends of similar wide artistic tastes. The double colonnades are the most striking feature of the exterior; inside there is a wealth of lavish ceilings and some particularly fine chimney-pieces and plasterwork. The gardens have an attractive classical Music Pavilion beside a cascade, and more classical statuary.

CAMBRIDGESHIRE

Anglesey Abbey, near Cambridge (NT)✲

One of the thirteenth-century abbeys dissolved by Henry VIII. Virtually rebuilt in the 1920s to house Lord Fairhaven's art collections. Everything is very good, but the bronzes and the gallery filled with paintings of Windsor Castle over 350 years are outstanding.

Wimpole Hall, near Cambridge (NT) (plate 9)

This splendid seventeenth-century house and garden are virtually a textbook compiled by many of Britain's leading architects, decorators and landscape designers. James Gibbs, James Thornhill, Henry Flitcroft and Sir John Soane all made major contributions. The designs of Charles Bridgeman and Capability Brown, a Gothic folly by Sanderson Miller and the unique feature of farm buildings by Soane make the grounds equally distinguished.

CHESHIRE

Gawsworth Hall, Macclesfield (plate 24)

An absolute gem, carefully restored and preserved by the present owners. Most of the structure is late fifteenth-century, evidenced externally by a garden front of superb half-timbering and internally by some magnificent exposed roof-trusses in the upstairs rooms. Full of good things inside, with a delightful lived-in atmosphere. In the grounds is one of the very rare surviving examples of a medieval tilting ground.

Little Moreton Hall, Congleton (NT)

The epitome of sixteenth-century half-timbered architecture: moated into the bargain.

Lyme Park, Disley (NT)*

Outside, one of the few houses designed by Leoni, in about 1720. Inside, parts of it are two hundred years older and include one of the finest large Elizabethan rooms in the British Isles, with plasterwork and panelling of great magnificence. Grinling Gibbons was here too.

Tatton Park, Knutsford (NT)*

Two of the Wyatts (Samuel and Lewis) built this large house around 1800. It is filled with good furniture and pictures; but more remarkable is the vast Tenants' Hall, built as late as 1935 for estate festivities and now full of extraordinary things from all over the world.

CORNWALL

Antony House, Torpoint (NT)

Practically unaltered since its erection between 1711 and 1721, and as a result an example of what a fine Queen Anne house should be. The contents match the structure, and show up particularly well against the panelling of the rooms.

Cotehele House, Calstock (NT)

Very important Tudor house, remarkable for being almost as it was when it was built. Particular features are the Great Hall, the roof very similar in style to the rather earlier one at Penshurst Place (page 63); and the chapel clock, unaltered and unmoved since 1489. The tapestries, furniture, armour and needlework have mostly been in the house for the last 250 years.

Lanhydrock, near Bodmin (NT)

One of the most splendid houses of the period (about 1640) though partly rebuilt after a fire in 1881. Make particularly for the fine gatehouse of 1658 and the great long gallery, 116 feet long with a plaster-panelled vaulted roof. The stone windows are interesting, with mullions but no transoms: they have a curiously modern look.

St. Michael's Mount, Penzance (NT)

One of the most romantic positions in Britain, still enough to pull one up short in spite of its familiarity. Architecturally a hotchpotch from medieval to Victorian, and inside a similar mixture with some particular features—the Chevy Chase Room containing a plasterwork frieze of hunting scenes (including ostriches), and the Gothic Revival Blue Rooms.

Tintagel, Old Post Office (NT)

A stately home by courtesy perhaps, having been a small fourteenth-century manor-house. It was a post office until the end of the nineteenth century. Architecturally of great interest, and conveniently situated in the middle of the village.

Trerice, St Newlyn East (NT) (plate 2)

Most attractive Elizabethan facade with particularly good curved gables to the roof. Dates from 1571 and contains fine plaster ceilings with pendants in the drawing room and the hall—which has a huge window of twenty-four sections.

CUMBRIA

Hill Top, near Sawrey (NT)

A seventeenth-century cottage, important to successive generations of children because Beatrix Potter lived and worked here. Full of Tiggy Winkle and Flopsy Bunny material, including many of her original watercolours.

Holker Hall, Cark-in-Cartmel ✲

Mostly Victorian, as the result of a huge fire which destroyed practically all of the earlier seventeenth-century house in 1871. The opportunity of rebuilding was used to create a grand mansion of red sandstone, all in Elizabethan style. When electricity was installed, the switches were hidden, often behind an imitation book with a punning title.

Levens Hall, Kendal ✽

There was an earlier building here, but practically everything one sees today dates from about 1580, when a new owner completely remodelled and refurnished the house. The exceedingly handsome plasterwork in the Hall and the Drawing Room is of this date, and the carved overmantels of the fireplaces in both the latter and the Small Drawing Room are of the highest quality. Throughout the house are pictures (including 'De Wint' drawings), furniture and silver of importance. Unique topiary gardens laid out in 1689.

Muncaster Castle, Ravenglass

Not quite what it seems, having been built in the 1860s on a medieval base. The castle is filled with a variety of objects which include some particularly fine seventeenth-century furniture and carvings, from Europe as well as Britain, and a series of outstanding chimney pieces of varying dates from Elizabethan to Georgian. There is a wonderful view over the Esk valley, and lovely walks in the terraced grounds.

DERBYSHIRE

Chatsworth, Bakewell ✽

One of the most stately of stately homes, known as the Palace of the Peak. Built between 1687 and 1707 by Talman, added to by Wyatville in the 1820s. The contents are outstanding by any standards—furniture, paintings, porcelain, books—and visitors should look at the Blue John ornaments particularly (it is locally mined). Ceilings by Verrio and others. There is an early nineteenth-century theatre, restored and used for changing exhibitions. In the huge grounds the long stepped water cascade and the fountains are features.

Haddon Hall, Bakewell (plate 4)✽

Largely unaltered, and regarded as the finest medieval house in the country. Many features are examples of their kind: the painted ceiling of about 1500 and the dated (1545) panelling in the dining room, the low, long gallery (early seventeenth-century), and the screen in the Hall (about 1450).

Hardwick Hall, near Chesterfield (NT) (plate 5)✽

An Elizabethan mansion of outstanding quality, climbing with its stone and glass towers towards the sky. Built for

Bess of Hardwick (Elizabeth, Countess of Shrewsbury) and filled with portraits, tapestries, furniture and needlework of her time; the alabaster chimney-pieces are particularly fine. The contemporary 12-feet high coloured frieze of hunting scenes in the High Great Chamber is unique.

Kedleston Hall, Derby

Thought to be Robert Adam's best, and practically untouched since it was built around 1760 on earlier foundations. The north front with its colonnade and pediment, and the south front (domed, with a double curved outside staircase) are matched by the interior. The Great Marble Hall is remarkable even in this magnificent house.

Melbourne Hall, Melbourne*

The origins of the house go back to the twelfth century, but the main (east) facade is a particularly handsome square, grey, pedimented example of early eighteenth-century work. The historic formal gardens are outstanding and contain one of Robert Bakewell's masterpieces in ironwork, the Birdcage.

Sudbury Hall, near Uttoxeter (NT)

All the best craftsmen of the age worked on this handsome seventeenth-century brick mansion — Grinling Gibbons, Edward Pierce (responsible for the curved balustrading to the staircase), the plasterers Bradbury and Pettifer (who created the ceilings in the staircase hall and the long gallery) and the painter Laguerre. The result is what has been called ' the richest series of Charles II rooms in the country '.

DEVONSHIRE

Arlington Court, Barnstaple (NT)

A particularly attractive Regency house built about 1820 to designs of Thomas Lee; square and white with a semi-circular balcony on pillars. Inside there are arches and pillars and galleries in pleasing proportions, and all sorts of unusual collections scattered throughout the house, including a room full of early pewter and lots of carriages in the stables.

Castle Drogo, Chagford (NT) (plate 25)

A Lutyens designed granite castle built between 1910 and 1930. The heroic conception and execution make full use of the dramatic position overlooking the 300-foot Teign gorge. The deliberately retained wild and open character of the long approach drive, the formal gardens sited well away from the castle and the somewhat austere interior continue to reflect the original intentions of architect and owner.

Killerton House and Gardens, near Exeter (NT)*

This estate which had as agent from 1808 the well-known nurseryman and landscape consultant John Veitch has been famous ever since for the choice planting of trees and shrubs. Nineteenth-century plant hunters sent their newly discovered seeds back to England and many arrived at Killerton to be tried out on the fifteen acres of sheltered hillside behind the house. Since 1977 Killerton House has been open to the public. The exterior is unremarkable but it conceals a sympathetically refurnished interior with excellent displays of costume arranged in natural groups in the rooms; themes and dresses are changed each season.

Powderham Castle, Kenton

This fortified manor-house, though considerably added to and altered in the eighteenth and nineteenth centuries, dates from about 1390. The later additions are castellated to match the original, and the skyline is a mass of towers, some of them part of the fourteenth-century house. Inside, the plasterwork of the Georgian staircase is particularly fine.

Saltram House, Plymouth (NT)

The main feature of this 1750 house, built round the core of a Tudor mansion, is the pair of rooms decorated by Robert Adam in 1768. These, with the fittings and carpets designed by him, are among Adam's greatest achievements. Elsewhere in the house are fine plasterwork and woodcarving, a major collection of porcelain, and a long series of Reynolds portraits. You can see all this by candlelight on certain evenings once a month: it is worth it.

DORSET

Athelhampton *

Medieval comfort at its most pleasant. The house was

largely built, in early Tudor times, from golden stone: both inside and out it has a peaceful rambling air. A splendid great hall, and lots of heraldic glass and linenfold panelling.

Forde Abbey, near Chard (plate 6)*

One of the ecclesiastical foundations (twelfth-century Cistercian) turned into a private house—but retaining almost uniquely the original abbey atmosphere in the Monks' Dormitory, the Undercroft and the Cloisters. Architecturally very important, and contains good plaster ceilings and tapestries.

Kingston Lacy, near Wimborne Minster (NT)

Built in 1663 for Sir Ralph Bankes and altered and enlarged by Sir Charles Barry in 1835, this mansion provides a fitting setting for the important pictures and furniture gathered by scholarly members of the family on their continental travels.

The Manor House, Sandford Orcas

Thought to be built by the same man as Athelhampton. A small manor-house reputedly filled with ghosts—men, women and dogs.

Sherborne Castle, Sherborne

Sir Walter Raleigh had the core of the castle built for him in 1594, and some of it still remains intact. Considerable additions and alterations in succeeding centuries have made it an architectural mixture, but it stands in a superb position on the edge of the lake. The interior is notable for the extremely handsome Gothic Revival library.

DURHAM

The Bowes Museum, Barnard Castle

Not actually a stately house but a museum; however it has many of the characteristics of a house and its conception in the 1860s (French-designed and intended to be built in France to house John Bowes's collections) was much more a domestic affair than a municipal one. An extraordinary, huge palace of a house, almost unbelievable in County Durham. Contents are outstanding—furniture, pictures, porcelain of the very best.

Raby Castle, Staindrop

Could never be mistaken for a country house. A fine castle, the origins of which go back to King Canute; most of the structure was built in about 1380, and it has scarcely changed since. The interior has been considerably redone, some of it in Victorian times, and the contents include good pictures and furniture. There is a collection of horse-drawn carriages.

EAST SUSSEX

Bateman's, Burwash (NT) *

Both a fine Jacobean country house (built 1634) and the Mecca of Rudyard Kipling fans. With the exception of one wing which no longer exists, the house is very largely original. Kipling lived here for 34 years, and many rooms—particularly the study where he wrote—are as he left them.

Firle Place, near Lewes

The contents match the exterior. Originally a fifteenth-century house, it was extensively altered in about 1730 to its present hipped and gabled medley. The Great Hall is still Tudor; the Staircase Hall is particularly fine with its plaster-work walls and ceiling. The pictures are very important, and there are excellent collections of Sèvres porcelain, and English and French furniture.

Glynde Place, near Lewes

Flint and brick (local materials) example of sixteenth-century architectural style; a most handsome result. The front is absolutely symmetrical with a central projecting porch and a rounded bay on each side. Pictures, bronzes and needlework inside.

Great Dixter, Northiam*

One of the few successful results of a twentieth-century architect working on a fifteenth-century house — Lutyens restored and added to the splendid half-timbered original in 1910. Huge, deeply projecting porch leads to a large and substantially intact Great Hall with a fine beamed roof over 30 feet high. Lutyens brought a complete extra sixteenth-century timber house from Kent and added it to the back: the marriage went exceptionally well.

Royal Pavilion, Brighton

The Prince Regent's extraordinary creation (to Nash's designs) for his country house by the sea. Restored to its full 1820 glories, and filled with most of the original furniture from the royal collections, the largely Chinese-style decorative schemes in the mainly Indian-style building produce an effect like nothing else in Britain — perhaps in the world.

ESSEX

Audley End House, Saffron Walden (plate 7)

James I is said to have remarked acidly that the Earl of Suffolk's new house was too large for a king though it might do for Lord Treasurer (which Suffolk was). Only a small part remains—which gives one an idea of its original vastness —and that is much changed. Original is the superb 1605 carved wooden hall screen. Vanbrugh made considerable alterations in the 1720s, Robert Adam decorated some rooms in the 1760s, and a good deal of Strawberry Hill Gothic was added about twenty years later. In spite of (or perhaps because of) the many hands, a splendid house.

Castle House, Dedham

The home of, and memorial to, that great painter of horses and other countryside matters, Sir Alfred Munnings. Over 100 of his paintings are on the walls of the house and studio.

GLOUCESTERSHIRE

Berkeley Castle ✶

An almost unique fortress built in 1153, largely remodelled inside between 1340 and 1380, and still inhabited by the same family. It is the oldest inhabited castle in England, and the scene of a good many unpleasantnesses including the murder of Edward II. A fine Great Hall, architectural details of the fourteenth century wherever you look, and a splendid position.

Sezincote, Moreton-in-Marsh*

This unique and enchanting house, finished in 1805, is a mixture of Hindu and Muslim architecture outside, with a classical Greek revival interior. It inspired the building of the Royal Pavilion at Brighton.

Snowshill Manor, Broadway (NT)

Tudor mainly, with a Queen Anne front (1700) success-fully disguising it. This architectural mixture houses a vast and extraordinary series of collections of such variety that a dozen visits will continue to unearth new material. Among them are lace-making equipment, musical instruments, model farm carts, toys and games, naval items, clocks, Japanese armour.

Sudeley Castle, Winchcombe*

Historically very important—six kings and queens of England have been through the gates, and the twelfth-century castle is particularly connected with Henry VIII and his wives. Apart from the particularly important collection of pictures and good tapestries and furniture, there is an exhibition (a type of internal *son-et-lumière*) which traces with sound and visual effects the history of the castle and its royal visitors.

HAMPSHIRE

Beaulieu Abbey and Palace House

Palace House is a mixture of fourteenth-century and late Victorian. The original abbey gateway was incorporated into the large extensions built in 1870; some of the original (though restored) fan vaulting can be seen today. The Abbey was, before the Dissolution in 1538, very large and important. Beaulieu offers a number of attractions to visitors, the major one being the famous National Motor Museum.

Breamore House, near Fordingbridge

Though considerably altered by rebuilding after a bad fire in 1856, Breamore retains most of its Elizabethan characteristics including a handsome E-shaped front (the wings are unusually shallow, projecting only the same amount as the porch) and several splendid fireplaces. There are, besides, a carriage museum and a countryside museum.

Broadlands, Romsey

A handsome eighteenth-century house visited by politicians, celebrities and royalty since it was built. Although the contents include fine Greek and Roman sculptures and rooms decorated by Robert Adam and Angelica Kauffmann, the majority of visitors now come to see the comprehensive memorial exhibition recording the long and varied career of the late owner, Lord Mountbatten of Burma.

Highclere Castle, near Newbury*

This vast 'Jacobethan' mansion was designed by Sir Charles Barry, architect of the Houses of Parliament, for the third Earl of Carnarvon. The display of ancient Egyptian artefacts found by the fifth Earl during his famous excavations of the tombs of the Pharaohs is in dramatic contrast to the opulent decoration and contents of the rest of the house.

Jane Austen's Home, Chawton

This is included for its associations with the novelist. The house is a pleasant brick building without any great distinction. Inside there is a collection of Jane Austen's possessions, and it has indeed been kept as it was when she lived and wrote there.

Stratfield Saye House, Reading (plate 19)

The home of the Dukes of Wellington since 1817, when it was presented to the Great Duke by a grateful nation. Architecturally based on a 1630 central core with Georgian and Victorian additions which add up to a harmonious whole. The interior is very much as it was when the first Duke lived there, and is filled with his possessions, acquisitions, and a selection from the vast amount of gifts presented to him by the sovereigns whose thrones he saved. There are outstanding samples of Sevres porcelain. Copenhagen, Wellington's horse which he rode at Waterloo, is buried in the grounds.

The Vyne, Basingstoke (NT)

Tucked away but very well worth reaching. It is something of an architectural mixture, but none the less a satisfying whole. The main part is Tudor, built from varying shades of red and purple bricks; the porticos on each side of the house were added about a hundred years later. The main features inside the house are the Oak Gallery, practically unique for its splendid carved panelling; and the staircase hall, a late eighteenth-century addition which comes as a considerable surprise in this home of Henry VIII's time.

HEREFORD AND WORCESTER

Eastnor Castle, near Ledbury

Pure nineteenth-century, designed by Robert Smirke, architect of the British Museum. Not his best effort, but it stands in lovely countryside, and the contents are in keeping with the romantic architecture.

Hellen's, Much Marcle

A quite small and unpretentious red brick manor-house, largely Jacobean but with earlier work incorporated; parts of the brickwork are from 1490, some of the earliest in Britain. Much of the interest of this house comes from the stories of its occupants, from Hetty Walwyn who went mad to Bloody Mary who didn't come after all.

HERTFORDSHIRE

Hatfield House (plate 10)*

This is a magnificent great Jacobean house built 1607-1612 by Robert Cecil (1st Earl of Salisbury) and the home of the Cecils ever since. It is full of splendid things, including relics of Queen Elizabeth I. The carved oak staircase is the finest seventeenth-century example in the country. In the grounds of Hatfield House is the remaining wing of the fifteenth-century Old Palace where Queen Elizabeth I spent several periods of her life. It has a fine original chestnut and oak ceiling under which Elizabethan banquets are once again regularly held.

Knebworth House

The external appearance of Knebworth is only skin deep, for the Victorian Gothic architecture covers up the remains of a Tudor house. The Banqueting Hall with its fine oak screen is of this period. The visitor passes abruptly from age to age however—the next room is Edwardian, by Lutyens, and there is a considerable amount of high Victorian furnishing and decoration. These parts of the house are full of the shades of Sir Edward Bulwer-Lytton and his friends.

Moor Park Mansion House

A Palladian villa, designed about 1727 (on an older house) partly by Leoni, the Italian architect who was also responsible for Clandon Park in Surrey. Many think this is his best work. The Great Hall particularly is rich and magnificent. Fine plasterwork, and decorations by (among others) Verrio.

Shaw's Corner, Ayot St. Lawrence (NT)

George Bernard Shaw lived here for over forty years until his death in 1950, and the whole house (of no architectural interest) is filled with his possessions and his personality.

HUMBERSIDE

Burton Agnes Hall, Bridlington

Great Elizabethan mansion house (about 1600) in warm red brick and an unusual style of architecture for the period; the very prominent bow windows filling all three storeys of each outer wing are about thirty years before their time. Many of the rooms are original, some with very fine plasterwork; the staircase and the Great Hall with its intricately carved screen and fireplace are also part of the original structure. Apart from much good furniture, panelling and china, there is an outstanding collection of French Impressionist pictures.

Burton Constable, near Hull

Basically an Elizabethan house, the centre block of which is externally much as it was in 1570; in the 1750s most of the additions were made, and the whole house was 'modernised' internally. Robert Adam and James Wyatt were among the architects invited to submit designs. Both did, but neither got the whole job. So the Great Hall and the Long Gallery are not Elizabethan as might appear, but mid-Georgian: and very delightful too with contents to match. All sorts of extras in the grounds—a country park, a pack of bloodhounds, a model railway.

Normanby Hall, Scunthorpe

Regency (actually 1825-29) house designed by Sir Robert Smirke, architect of the British Museum, and costing £29,726 to build—the original account books survive. Carefully refurnished and redecorated in period.

Sledmere House, Driffield *

Built in three stages: a central square block in 1751, followed by two large wings at right angles in 1781-8, and finally a partial reconstruction after a fire in 1911. The alterations and improvements are exceptionally well integrated with the original house. Inside there is some delightful plasterwork in all the main rooms. The finest room is the long Library on the first floor which spans the whole length of the South front.

Wilberforce House, Hull

This late Elizabethan town house was severely mauled in the 1730s and later, but its principal interest lies in the association with William Wilberforce. He was born here, and devoted his whole life to the abolition of slavery. The house is filled with relics and mementoes of him. There is also a series of quasi-period rooms, from Elizabethan to Victorian.

ISLE OF WIGHT

Arreton Manor, Arreton

Mainly late Elizabethan; a small manor-house of pale grey stone, showing the E shape characteristic of many houses of the period. Apart from the expected features (panelling, furniture, fireplaces) inside, there is a notable collection of dolls and other children's items.

Carisbrooke Castle

Its principal claim to fame is the imprisonment there of Charles I for nearly a year; there are relics of his stay. The castle is a real one, built and added to in the twelfth, thirteenth and fourteenth centuries. Very well looked after by the Department of the Environment and still largely complete, it provides plenty to see including a sixteenth-century well-house where donkeys work the mechanism for raising the water.

Osborne House (plate 8)

Queen Victoria's favourite country house, mainly designed by Prince Albert. The large mansion is not only the epitome of Victorian taste in the general sense, but is filled to bursting point with all the things which Victoria and Albert held most dear. It is evocative and nostalgic, and one feels how happy they were there.

KENT

Boughton Monchelsea Place, near Maidstone

An architectural mixture with Regency additions (including battlements) to an Elizabethan manor house. The material used is Kentish ragstone, quarried very close by. A most pleasant lived-in atmosphere greets the visitor when he can tear himself away from the staggering views of the Weald. The staircase of about 1690 is a good example.

Chartwell, Westerham (NT)✻

Surprisingly, Sir Winston Churchill's house dates mainly from the 1920s, having been almost completely rebuilt from the ugly Victorian mansion that it was. Preserves the spirit of its famous owner as few other 'association' houses do, mainly because of his diverse talents—his paintings in the garden studio, the brick walls he built and the books he wrote there all add to the aura of Britain's Bulldog.

Chiddingstone Castle, near Edenbridge

In what is claimed to be the prettiest village in Kent (all the rest of which is owned by the National Trust). The house only became a castle in the early nineteenth century, before which it was called High Street House. Inside, much of the 1679 house remains; it contains collections of Stuart relics and Japanese, Egyptian and Buddhist items.

Godinton Park, Ashford ✻

A very handsome red brick house, mostly of about 1630 but with earlier and later parts and details. The magnificent Great Chamber which occupies much of the first floor is full of splendid panelling and carving and contains an equally impressive chimney-piece.

Hever Castle, near Edenbridge ✻

From the outside, probably the best example of a fortified manor-house of the fifteenth century—some of it is even a good deal earlier. It was the home of Anne Boleyn, Henry VIII's second wife. The interior, with some exceptions including the moulded beams in Henry VIII's room, is almost entirely Edwardian, created after the castle had been bought in 1903 by William Waldorf Astor. Given that it had crumbled internally to a sad state of dereliction, he did a marvellous job of modernised restoration.

Ightham Mote, Ivy Hatch (NT)

Another Kentish ragstone building, one of the best-preserved and most complete medieval manor-houses in the country, surrounded by a moat. Parts of the building are early fourteenth century, and much of the remainder, including the exceptional chapel, about 1500.

Knole, Sevenoaks (NT)

Certainly one of the largest and most magnificent palaces (it can hardly be called a house) in Britain. Based on a core of about 1460, and much extended from 1603 after Elizabeth I had given it to the Sackvilles. There are many famous state rooms—the Venetian Ambassador's Room, the King's Bedroom, the Cartoon Gallery—all filled with furniture, pictures and other objects of unparalleled richness. Outstanding even among these are the silver furniture and the tapestries of the King's Bedroom, furnished for James I.

Leeds Castle, Maidstone

Tapestries, pictures and furniture are worthy of a building which castle experts consider to be 'the loveliest castle in the world'. In an inccmparable setting surrounded by water and park, this was the much loved dower castle for eight of England's medieval queens.

Penshurst Place, Tunbridge Wells *

Largely fourteenth-century, and excellently preserved. The Great Hall, built about 1340, is the model for all others and the house, including its Elizabethan additions, is full of material of great historical and artistic interest. Its own long history is woven into the story of England. A recent addition is a comprehensive toy museum.

Squerryes Court, Westerham

An example of the square, formal, uncluttered architecture of 1680, when Sir Christopher Wren's influence was felt everywhere. The hipped roof, dormer windows and strict proportions are quite typical. The pictures and furniture are largely contemporary with the house. There is also a collection of pictures and items associated with General Wolfe, who is further commemorated by a cenotaph in the garden.

Walmer Castle, Walmer*

Built by Henry VIII in 1539 to protect his ships from the French, and shows the grim gun-ports through the enormously thick walls. The castle was converted inside in 1730 for rather more comfortable living than it had originally been designed for. The process has been continued by each successive Lord Warden of the Cinque Ports, for whom this has been the official residence since the early 1700s. The Duke of Wellington (a Warden) died here, and mementoes of his stay and death are displayed.

LANCASHIRE

Browsholme Hall, near Clitheroe

Browsholme Hall (pronounced locally as Brews'em) is a lop-sided, three-storeyed stone house to which successive generations of the Parker family have made additions since its original building in the early 1500s. The huge Tudor Hall is filled with an astonishing variety of objects ranging from a fifteenth-century dog gauge to a piece of Zeppelin. Much of the rest of the house contains displays of exceptional interest—pictures, furniture, china, glass and others — against a background of a wide variety of splendid panelling.

Leighton Hall, Carnforth (plate 23)

This little Regency mock castle lies at the bottom of a great curved bowl of landscape, and looks in some lights as if it has been painted there on the backcloth of the Lakeland mountains. Inside, there is the best kind of Gothic revival architecture — graceful and imaginative — as a background to a unique collection of splendid furniture from the Gillows of Lancaster, whose family home this is.

LEICESTERSHIRE

Belvoir Castle, near Grantham

Several of the Wyatt family had a hand in the building of this eighteenth and nineteenth-century romantic castle, which sits perched on a hill and dominates the countryside for miles around. There was a castle there before, but fires have left little of it. A great deal of arms and armour decorate the stone corridors and landings. There is an eighteenth-century Chinese room and a sumptuous Elizabethan (i.e. nineteenth-century Elizabethan) saloon among other splendours.

LINCOLNSHIRE

Belton House, Grantham

One of the few country houses confidently attributed to Sir Christopher Wren—though doubts remain. At all events, an extremely handsome building of 1685 in golden-grey stone; and the interior is one of the finest in the country with Grinling Gibbons carvings in many of the ground-floor rooms, a Chinese bedroom, a 1780 library by Wyatt, and splendid furniture, tapestries, china and pictures throughout. There is also a collection of items connected with the Duke of Windsor.

Burghley House, Stamford

The biggest and grandest Elizabethan mansion in England. William III remarked: 'This house is too large for a subject.' Based on a monastery, it was completed in 1589 since when it has remained, in all essentials, unaltered. Grinling Gibbons carvings, a superb collection of paintings, outstanding tapestries, and Verrio's masterpiece the Heaven Room, considered to be the finest painted room in the country; his other ceilings in the house are of equal magnificence.

Doddington Hall, Doddington

Strikingly impressive in its three-storeyed regularity, this Elizabethan mansion is exactly as it was designed in 1593 and completed in 1660. The interior is quite different, having been completely redone in 1761. The contents include a good collection of porcelain and furniture.

The Old Hall, Gainsborough

The building has been through some stormy times before coming into the careful and sensitive hands of the Friends of the Old Hall Association; at various times it has been a pub, a linen factory, a Masonic temple, a theatre and a Congregational church. It was originally a manor-house, built in the fifteenth century with sixteenth-century additions, and its fine half-timbering and brickwork (very little stone in Lincolnshire) remains remarkably intact.

LONDON

Apsley House

The Duke of Wellington's house (sometimes known as No. 1 London) and since 1947 a museum of the great Duke's life and possessions. The house has the added distinction of being designed by Robert Adam, though the original red brick of 1778 was covered with stone in 1830, when considerable extensions were also made. A wealth of gifts from grateful monarchs is on display.

Chiswick House (plate 11)*

Most of the important names in seventeenth and eighteenth-century architecture were involved in the conception and construction of Chiswick House. Based on Palladio's work in Italy, designed by Lord Burlington (and built 1727-30), decorated by William Kent (who also laid out the garden), added to by James Wyatt. The many hands have made exceptionally light work.

Ham House (NT)

Originally built in 1610 in the form of an H, and altered several times during the same century (but not substantially after that). A very important example of Stuart architecture, and an equally important collection of contemporary furnishings—much of it original to the house, and supported by the seventeenth-century inventories.

Hampton Court Palace *

Vast royal (though not now used by the royal family) palace of dark red brick. It was originally a priory, and was bought by Cardinal Wolsey in 1514; he built such a splendid palace, including the Great Gatehouse, for himself that Henry VIII appropriated it for his own use. He made some additions (notably the Great Hall), but the next major rebuilding was done from 1689 onwards, under the control of Christopher Wren. Grinling Gibbons carvings are much in evidence. Magnificent state rooms.

Kensington Palace *

Wren designed parts of this palace for William and Mary between 1689 and 1695. William Kent did the rest for George I between 1718 and 1726. The State Apartments show the differences. There are Grinling Gibbons carvings in the King's Gallery.

Kenwood (The Iveagh Bequest)

The epitome of the Neo-Classic style with its finely proportioned four-pillared pediment for all the world like a converted Greek temple. Robert Adam was responsible for this from 1764 onwards. The house contains the very important Iveagh Bequest of paintings, including all the most famous names from Rembrandt to Turner.

Marble Hill House, Twickenham

Handsomely situated beside the Thames at Twickenham, this classically proportioned small house owes everything to Palladian ideas but actually seems to have been designed by comparative unknowns, including one noble amateur. Completed in 1729 and scarcely touched since. The furnishings are contemporary.

Osterley Park House (NT)✳

One of Robert Adam's great successes; the work of converting the Elizabethan house to his classical ideas lasted from 1761 to 1780. The interior is 'all delicacy, gaiety, grace and beauty' (in his own words), achieved by the furniture which he designed throughout as well as the architecture and decorations.

Syon House, Brentford (plate 16)✳

Adam was doing up this sixteenth-century house at the same time as Osterley Park (see above), and here too he was responsible for nearly everything—carpets, furniture, decorative schemes. The style is more magnificent than at Osterley, with lavish and grandiose effects created by pillars and columns and marbled floors. The Long Gallery, 136 feet long but only 14 feet wide, was Adam's special pride.

MERSEYSIDE

Speke Hall, Liverpool (NT)

Eye-dazzling, black-and-white, half-timbered Elizabethan manor-house, practically unaltered, surrounding a courtyard. The immediate proximity of Liverpool's busy airport does not detract from its romantic atmosphere. A lot of splendid plasterwork, chimney-pieces and carving; and the whole house is riddled with spy holes and secret spaces from the days of religious persecution.

NORFOLK

Blickling Hall, Aylsham (NT)*

The first sight of this handsome golden-reddish seventeenth-century house, all pinnacles, gables and chimneys at the end of its tunnel of clipped hedges and contemporary outbuildings, is entirely unexpected. Inside, much of the work is mid to late eighteenth-century. The Long Gallery is something of a monster, with a very fine Jacobean plaster ceiling supported by unfortunate Victorian Gothic oak bookcases and a deep frieze of painted patterns created at the same time. The visitor should not be put off—the rest is splendid.

Felbrigg Hall, near Cromer (NT)

Miles from anywhere but well worth finding. The two main aspects of the house, set corner to corner, look as if they might have met by accident. One is pure 1620s, projecting mullioned windows, curly gables, tall clusters of chimneys. The other is pure 1680s, square, serene, uncluttered, with a row of little dormer windows. How tastes changed in sixty years! The interior was considerably altered at later dates. Some fine Jacobean plasterwork and good furniture and paintings, including a room full of pictures brought back from the Grand Tour, and a Gothic Revival library.

Holkham Hall, Wells *

Some authorities think this is the most beautiful house in England. This is certainly not true of the exterior, which is yellow, oddly windowed and somewhat forbidding. The inside is a revelation, however. ' Coke of Norfolk' (the owner), Lord Burlington and William Kent between them created a magnificence which is as effective today as it was in the 1730s. The Marble Hall is almost beyond description, and the other rooms on view are quite outstanding.

Oxburgh Hall, Swaffham (NT)

Fifteenth-century brickwork at its best. The magnificent gatehouse with its double towers 80 feet high, castellated and unevenly windowed, lies on the other side of a proper, water-filled moat which surrounds the whole house. This was more symbolic than necessary at this date (1482).

NORTHAMPTONSHIRE

Althorp, Northampton

The original structure dates from medieval times, but a whole series of major alterations at regular intervals, culminating in a final effort of 1790, result in what one sees today. The interior is very fine, with handsome and sumptuous rooms filled with a particularly important collection of pictures and china.

Castle Ashby, Northampton *

Another Elizabethan house, almost contemporary with Burghley, Cambs, but built in a very different style with its flat-topped towers and four-square look. Inigo Jones was responsible for the front (1635). One of its exterior features is the long quotation in Latin, worked in the form of a stone parapet round the top of the house, from the 127th Psalm. The interior contains particularly fine panelling and staircases from the seventeenth century, and furniture and pictures of the same period.

Lamport Hall, Northampton

Lamport Hall opened for the first time in 1974. A good deal of rebuilding has been done by successive generations of the Isham family since the mid-sixteenth century. One of the main restylings was completed in 1655 under the direction of Inigo Jones's son-in-law, John Webb. The identical wings which flank Webb's south-west front were designed by Francis Smith of Warwick, and built in the 1730s. There is fine eighteenth-century plasterwork inside, particularly in the Staircase Hall and the Music Hall.

Rockingham Castle, near Corby

Fortified by William the Conqueror soon after 1066; he and his successors for five hundred years used it frequently as a royal residence. In 1530 it came into the Watson family, who still live there. The alterations and improvements to the house through nine hundred years have blended surprisingly well, and the result is an unexpectedly comfortable house full of the atmosphere of English history.

Sulgrave Manor, Banbury

George Washington's ancestral home, and consequently a shrine for Americans visiting Britain. Originally Tudor (parts remain) with Elizabethan and later additions and alterations. Lots of interesting Washingtoniana.

NORTHUMBERLAND

Alnwick Castle, Alnwick

Very little changed in plan since its construction in the twelfth century as a bastion against the Scots. Various military alterations were made through the centuries to keep up with modern methods of warfare (the main gateway and the Barbican are important examples of fifteenth-century brickwork). Finally (as he thought) Robert Adam was brought in to make the interior comfortable and elegant which he did between 1755 and 1766 in Gothic revival style. A hundred years later most of this was swept away and redone in Italian Renaissance style. The effect of this protracted hotchpotch of styles is, surprisingly, very pleasing.

Cragside, Rothbury (NT)

Built by a local millionaire industrialist, Cragside epitomises the best in Victorian architecture (Norman Shaw), furniture (Gillows of Lancaster) and decoration (William Morris). It is an important and remarkably complete survival from a period which has until recently been underestimated and neglected.

Lindisfarne Castle, Holy Island (NT)

Romantically sited on top of a crag on Holy Island off the bleak Northumberland coast (it is cut off at high tide). A fort against the Scots was built in the 1540s, and was used until the early nineteenth century for a garrison. Left more or less empty for a hundred years it was then restored by Sir Edwin Lutyens to its present condition. The warren of small rooms and steep staircases, at several levels, makes an almost unique house. The walls are happily thick enough to keep out the North Sea gales.

Seaton Delaval Hall, near Newcastle-on-Tyne

The last great house (1718-1729) built by Vanbrugh, standing bleak and brooding in an unlikely setting between industrial Blyth and the North Sea. A central block with two huge wings projecting forward at right angles. A series of major fires seriously damaged much of the interior.

Wallington Hall, Cambo (NT)*

Externally rather forbidding with its stone-block regularity, unchanged since its erection was started in 1688. The inside was almost certainly in keeping, until an owner in the middle of the eighteenth century decided to make it more elegant. Italian plasterers were given free rein, and local architects and craftsmen were largely employed. The result is an exceedingly comfortable small house, filled with the things which a well-off (but not super-rich) family collected together in the Georgian period. Particularly good china. The garden is about half a mile away through the woods—a Scottish habit.

NORTH YORKSHIRE

Beningbrough Hall, near Shipton (NT)

Long-fronted, two storeyed house built in narrow bricks, with stone corners. It dates from about 1716; various guesses as to who designed it have ruled out Vanbrugh and come down in favour of a local man, Thomas Archer. Many minor alterations have taken place inside, but it remains a fine example of provincial country-house architecture.

Castle Howard, York (plate 21)

Vanbrugh's colossal palace (it would have been Talman's but for a row between Lord Carlisle and the architect) erected between 1700 and about 1726; the west wing was added a quarter of a century later in a totally different style. The scale of Castle Howard is immense, both inside and out. The pictures, furniture, tapestries, porcelain, statuary and decorations would all be of major importance in almost any other house; here they are overshadowed by the ornate magnificence of the building.

Newby Hall, Ripon ✤

Comparatively small but particularly charming brick country house, mainly about 1705 with alterations and additions by Robert Adam between 1765 and 1783 (the great stable block is his). The Tapestry Room by Adam, designed to display a magnificent set of Gobelins tapestries, is one of his happiest creations: ceilings by Zucchi. The Sculpture Gallery is, if possible, even better.

Ripley Castle, Ripley

Ripley Castle is an amalgam of sixteenth and eighteenth century architecture, and contains in the older part some fine rooms of the period. Among these are the Tower Room, with its unfussy panelling and vine scroll plasterwork ceiling; and the Knight's Chamber, the wagon roof of which is an important survival.

NOTTINGHAMSHIRE

Newstead Abbey, Linby ✤

An Augustinian priory until Henry VIII dealt with the monasteries; some of the thirteenth-century abbey remains. The Byron family built a house in 1540, and its main interest now is its association with the poet who lived here from 1808 (by which time the house was in a state of decay). Many Byron relics.

OXFORDSHIRE

Blenheim Palace, Woodstock ✻

Vanbrugh's huge palace for the Duke of Marlborough, similar in scale to his other vast house, Castle Howard. Built between 1704 and 1716, its cost (largely because of Vanbrugh's extravagant ideas) was a constant source of friction between Duchess and architect; in the end he left in a rage. It is hardly possible to pick out individual parts for mention—the whole is more important than the parts, and that whole needs to be looked at in relation to the equally huge and carefully designed park. Sir Winston Churchill was born here.

Broughton Castle, Banbury

One of the most delightful situations for any castle—an accident of nature, since it was chosen for defence in the fourteenth century. The castle was built in Decorated style, and major additions were made in Elizabeth I's reign, marrying up very happily. Very good plasterwork inside. Unlike Chastleton House (see below) this was a Roundhead stronghold in the Civil War, and a number of relics remain. There is an unusual interior porch in the panelled drawing room.

Buscot Park, near Faringdon (NT)

Delightful 1780 house filled with eighteenth-century furniture of the highest quality and paintings by Rubens, Rembrandt and Jordaens. An unusual feature is the Briar Rose room—the walls covered with a series of Burne-Jones paintings done in 1890.

Chastleton House, Moreton-in-Marsh

This splendid Cotswold mansion has been occupied by the same family ever since it was built at the beginning of the seventeenth century. Strong associations with the Royalist cause have left some unique souvenirs: Charles I's bible that he used on the scaffold, Jacobite glass. Important contemporary panelling, and an astonishing plaster ceiling to the Ballroom (in fact a long gallery).

Greys Court, Henley-on-Thames (NT)

The sixteenth-century house was largely rebuilt in Georgian times, but the surrounding ruins are part of the original fourteenth-century fortifications, and the whole agglomeration of buildings stands on a romantic hill-top site. In the stables there is a Tudor donkey wheel in working order.

Mapledurham House

Fine Elizabethan mansion picturesquely situated on the side of the Thames, happily restored (a continuing process) from what appeared a few years ago to be an irreversible process of decay. The small road goes no further than the banks of the river and it is easy to people the remote and attractive setting with figures from the past.

Milton Manor House, near Abingdon

Said to be one of Inigo Jones's with Georgian expansions. In this severely elegant mansion one finds, surprisingly, a library and chapel of pure Strawberry Hill Gothic.

Rousham House, Steeple Aston *

The main structure is 1635, and unmistakably so with its thrusting E shape. In the 1730s William Kent designed new wings (which are comparatively unobtrusive), decorated most of the inside and also laid out the gardens—his only landscape design still in existence.

Stonor Park, near Henley-on-Thames

Few privately owned houses have such strong historical claims to a visit as Stonor: eight hundred years in the same family and a Catholic stronghold where Edmund Campion, the sixteenth-century Jesuit martyr, had his secret room with printing press. Contents range from fine bronzes to the charming shell bed supported by mermaids on a silvery sea.

SALOP

Attingham, near Shrewsbury (NT)

This was the grandest house in the county when it was built in the 1780s. Nash did alterations and improvements some thirty years later. The style is classical, with three decreasing storeys in a square facade, and a huge pediment perched on top of four very thin columns. The interior is splendid, with a be-columned entrance hall, attractive plasterwork in several of the rooms, and two particularly good rooms, typical of the period, in the Octagon and the Round Room.

Stokesay Castle, Craven Arms

Unique in being the oldest fortified house (in spite of its name it was a house, not a fortress) in England. The Great Hall (the main part of the house) was built in about 1270, and stands behind its moat today much as it did then. Little inside is later than Elizabethan, and some of the panelling and fireplaces are specially good. Although unfurnished, Stokesay's atmosphere and architectural interest justify its inclusion here.

Weston Park, near Shifnal ✻

Large and splendid mansion built in the 1670s and sited in a beautiful park created at a later date. The important contents include an excellent collection of paintings, together with very good tapestries and furniture. Disraeli paid many visits, and a large number of his letters are displayed.

SOMERSET

Dunster Castle

Perched on a wooded hilltop, some of the original structure of this thirteenth-century fortification still remains (particularly the Gateway) but much of it was remodelled in late Victorian times. There are additions and alterations at many dates in between, but the whole is remarkably unified. Two particular features of the interior are the plaster ceiling of the Dining Room, an outstanding work of seventeenth-century craftsmanship; and the handsome carved elm staircase of 1681, which although not Grinling Gibbons's work is as good as anything he did.

Gaulden Manor, Tolland, near Taunton*

This is a sixteenth-century manor house of immense charm with unexpectedly elaborate plaster ceilings and friezes in the Great Hall and adjoining Chapel.

Montacute House, Yeovil (NT)

Beautiful tall house of golden stone, completed in about 1600 in the traditional E shape. Unusually, some *earlier* additions were made (in 1786) by importing a Gothic porch from an older house. Inside, there is a huge long gallery (189 feet long) among other pure Elizabethan delights.

STAFFORDSHIRE

Shugborough, Great Haywood (NT)

The square, formal, regular house was started in 1693, added to in the 1760s, remodelled again between 1790 and 1806 to the designs of Samuel Wyatt, and finally altered (somewhat to the detriment of the whole concept) in the 1920s. Most of the furniture and pictures are handsome without being of national importance. The Staffordshire County Museum is housed (extremely well) in part of the house. The grounds contain important monuments and statuary, some of them the first to be seen in England in the neo-Greek style that arrived in about 1762.

SUFFOLK

Ickworth, near Bury St Edmunds (NT) (plate 12)

An architectural freak, if such a word can be used for this imposing mansion of 1795 onwards. In the middle, an enormous rotunda with domed roof and pedimented porch on four columns; from each side a curving corridor with a square bulge half way down; and at the end of each curve a complete wing, originally designed to house the owner's collections of pictures and sculptures respectively. The rotunda has the main rooms (one a huge half-circle) and one of the bulges in the corridor is a fine Pompeian room. Splendid pictures, statuary and furniture throughout.

Kentwell Hall, Long Melford

A classic example of a red brick Tudor mansion probably completed before 1563. Externally it survives almost intact with moat, projecting wings and staircase turrets but inside visitors see all stages of a remarkable restoration programme started only in 1972.

Melford Hall, near Sudbury (NT)

Imposing two-storeyed red brick mansion with tall octagonal towers ending in onion-shaped domes. Built between 1554 and 1578, the exterior is substantially the same today except for a connecting wing. Inside there is an attractive Regency library, but the remainder is largely Elizabethan; there is a contemporary stained-glass portrait window of Queen Bess herself on the staircase (she really did stay here).

Somerleyton Hall, near Lowestoft ✤

Although built on a sixteenth-century shell, this is a Victorian house and proud of it. Extravagantly created in red brick and stone in almost equal proportions, the 1857 structure was the fulfilment of a railway tycoon's dream; he went bankrupt a few years later. There is an exceptional maze in the grounds.

SURREY

Clandon Park, near Guildford (NT)

A fairly recent addition to the houses open to the public, and worth waiting for. The house, one of Leoni's few works in this country and an example of Palladian architecture at its most elegant, has been restored to its full glory. The Marble Hall is an outstanding room by any standards; the Palladio room and the Saloon are a delight to the eye. The house provides a fitting home for the important Gubbay collection of furniture, pictures, pottery and porcelain.

Hatchlands, East Clandon (NT)

The money for building this plain deep-red brick Palladian house in 1756 came from the admiral owner's prize-money. The interior is historic simply because it was Robert Adam's first commission after his return from Italy, at the age of thirty; he had to work on someone else's structure, and the results understandably are rather tentative compared with his later masterpieces.

Loseley House, near Guildford (plate 13)

Elizabethan house *par excellence*. The apparent regularity of the front proves, on closer inspection, to be extremely deceptive; nothing matches at all. The result is very attractive. There is fine panelling, splendid ceilings, one monumental sixteenth-century fireplace, and much contemporary furniture and decoration.

Polesden Lacey, near Dorking (NT) ✤

In a wonderful setting looking across the valley to the Downs. The house is of no age, being a combination of an 1824 villa and a major extension and refurbishing in 1906. The interior is a great mixture of styles, from severe mock Jacobean to sumptuous mock Louis XIV. The quality of work is very high throughout, and the result is a great success. Contents to match with particularly good pictures.

WARWICKSHIRE

Baddesley Clinton (NT)

The survival of this remarkable moated manor is due both to its seclusion and to the dedication of generations of the Ferrers family. The stone front and rear wings date from 1300 and 1450 and combine to produce an almost perfect example of late medieval domestic architecture. The interior is equally important; with its panelling, splendid carved fireplaces and early furniture it remains virtually unchanged since 1634.

Charlecote Park, Warwick (NT)

Shakespeare is said to have poached a deer in the park of this expansive 1550 red brick mansion. The gatehouse is even earlier, and remains quite unaltered. The main house is E-shaped with octagonal domed towers; considerable alterations were made in the nineteenth century, both inside and out, and though impressive, little of the interior remains as it was.

Coughton Court, Alcester (NT)

The magnificent central gatehouse is dated 1509 and has towers, battlements and a fine oriel window. In one of its rooms the wives of the Gunpowder plotters awaited the results of the first Guy Fawkes night. The two enclosing wings are half-timbered, also of early sixteenth-century date. Considerable alterations and additions (and some deletions from earlier changes) took place at later dates, and the interior of the house is a mixture of style; there is very good panelling, unusually combining wood and marble, of about 1740 in the Dining Room and the Tribune adjoining.

Packwood House, Hockley Heath (NT) *

One of the main features is not architectural but the Yew Garden, created in about 1670 and representing the Sermon on the Mount—Master, Evangelists, Apostles, multitude and all. The house is earlier (about 1550) but added to at the time of the Yew Garden and altered in both the eighteenth and nineteenth centuries. It is filled with good early furniture and tapestries.

Ragley Hall, Alcester (plate 17)

One of the handsomest classical Georgian houses in the Midlands. The architect of the main structure (1680 onwards) was Robert Hooke, an associate of Wren when the latter was building churches throughout the City of London; the great portico to the main entrance was added by Wyatt in 1800. The main glory of the interior is the Great Hall, a stunning creation in plasterwork by James Gibbs in 1750. Elsewhere there are Grinling Gibbons carvings, good pictures and fine china throughout.

Upton House, Edgehill (NT)

Although the main part of the house is based on a core of the late seventeenth century and important as such, it is overshadowed by the splendour of the pictures and porcelain collections displayed within. The pictures include works by Rembrandt, Rubens, Stubbs, Cuyp and Gainsborough; the porcelain is largely Sèvres with some very important Chelsea. There are also superb tapestries.

Warwick Castle, Warwick *

The castle walls fall vertically down to the Avon, as they have done since about 1345. Caesar's Tower and the gateway date from this time; Guy's Tower from 1394. After two hundred years it had fallen into a state of decay (part of it was the county gaol), but was restored with the aid of a grant from James I; since then it has scarcely altered. The interior is much later (eighteenth and nineteenth centuries largely) but very sumptuous, with rich furnishings and some important pictures (Holbein and Rubens among them). There are also dungeons and an armoury to see. The grounds are an oasis of peace if you avoid the rush hours and high season.

WEST MIDLANDS

Aston Hall, Birmingham

Astonishingly set in the middle of an industrial suburb of Birmingham, this is none the less an authentic, excellently preserved and imaginatively run (by Birmingham Museum) Jacobean manor-house built 1618-35. The Long Gallery, Great Stairs, Great Drawing Room (with a notable plaster ceiling) and several other rooms are largely original, and have been furnished to match.

Wightwick Manor, Wolverhampton (NT) (plate 3)

Edward Ould was the distinguished architect responsible in 1887 for providing the setting, and the firm of William Morris and Company for the interior decoration. The influence of the Pre-Raphaelite movement and their contemporaries is evident in every room: in wallpapers, upholstery, curtains and carpets; De Morgan tiles surround the fireplaces and volumes from the Kelmscott Press fill the bookshelves; drawings and watercolours by Burne-Jones, Ford Madox Brown, Millais and Rossetti hang on the Morris wallpaper. The preservation of this remarkable interior is due to the donor, the leading expert on the subject.

WEST SUSSEX

Arundel Castle, Arundel

Although there are Norman beginnings to this huge castle, little early work remains. The twin Barbican Towers, reached by a bridge over the moat, were erected in 1295; the Keep is even older. Practically all the visitor sees inside is Victorian, in Gothic style. One of the best parts is from a slightly earlier rebuilding in Regency times; the Library, 117 feet long with galleries all along, is an excellent example of attractive Gothic revival. The Castle, largely Victorianised as it may be, is none the less full of lovely things—the pictures in particular.

Goodwood House, Chichester (plate 14)

In a lovely setting near the Sussex coast. The design is mainly James Wyatt's, built (but not completed: one wing was never constructed) between 1790 and 1800. The material is again the local flint, plus stone. Wyatt worked on another architect's beginnings and the combined operations have not perhaps resulted in his very best work. But the Tapestry Room is a masterpiece. Some very attractive pictures and sculpture, and excellently displayed porcelain.

Parham, Pulborough*

A particularly fine and well-preserved Elizabethan house of grey stone, which although considerably altered in the eighteenth and nineteenth centuries has since been largely 'unaltered' again. The interior has retained its original character for almost exactly four hundred years, and contains very good plaster ceilings and contemporary pictures, needlework and furniture.

Petworth House, Petworth (NT) (plate 15)

A wide range of periods is represented in the buildings: the Chapel is thirteenth-century, the main house about 1680, with considerable alterations in about 1870. The contents are of national importance, among them a Grinling Gibbons room decorated throughout with the master-carver's creations in limewood; a Turner room with thirteen pictures by England's most famous painter (he was a frequent visitor); an eighteenth-century sculpture gallery almost unique in the country; and a wealth of splendid pictures throughout the house.

Uppark, near Petersfield (NT)

Aptly named, the house stands at the top of a considerable hill. It was designed by William Talman (who also created Dyrham Park near Bristol) and built in 1685-90 from red brick with stone facings. It is absolutely typical of the Wren-style country house, square and formal and uncluttered. The inside of the house was completely redecorated in the middle of the eighteenth century, and has since remained almost untouched—and splendid to see—with most of its original furnishings.

WEST YORKSHIRE

Brontë Parsonage Museum, Haworth

The Brontë home, a comfortable smallish house on the edge of the Yorkshire moors. Most of the novels and poems, including *Wuthering Heights* and *Jane Eyre* were written here. Full of atmosphere as well as relics of the family.

Harewood House ✻

One of Robert Adam's, overlying the original efforts of a local architect. His hand is seen throughout the house, unifying the proportions, decorative schemes and furnishings of practically every room. Sir Charles Barry was allowed to make Victorian improvements in some of them (the Gallery and the Library in particular). Particularly rich in Chippendale furniture of superb quality (the wooden pelmets in the Gallery are his too), and there is a wealth of pictures and porcelain too.

Nostell Priory, Wakefield (NT) (plate 20)

Originally, of course, a real priory until shut down by Henry VIII in the 1530s. The present house was begun in 1733, and it was designed by nineteen-year-old James Paine, whose name it made (he went on to do some of Chatsworth, Kedleston and Wardour Castle). But here again, Robert Adam was called in later. Both men contributed almost equally to the fine interiors, employing Zucchi and Angelica Kauffmann for ceilings and murals, and Chippendale for the furniture. One of the chief glories of Nostell is the Chippendale furniture, complete with practically all the original bills. He was born nearby.

WILTSHIRE

Longleat House, Warminster ✻

One of the most impressive (and impressively situated) houses in the country. Its three-tiered grey stone bulk stands in the middle of a magnificent stretch of unspoiled countryside, and must look much the same as it did when it was completed in about 1580. With the exception of the Great Hall, which contains original work in the form of the hammerbeams of the roof and the fireplace, practically everything inside the house is of Regency or Victorian date. Nevertheless, many of the rooms are sumptuous in their decorations. Among the superb contents is a magnificent collection of books, part of which is contained in the 1878 Red Library.

Mompesson House, Salisbury (NT)

A town house in the Close surrounding Salisbury Cathedral

completed in 1701 and a small gem of Wren's style (though not by his hand). A good deal of redecoration (including elaborate plasterwork, fireplaces and overmantels in the main rooms) was done in about 1740, and a new wing was added. The result is a particularly happy and effective blend.

Sheldon Manor, Chippenham

To list the architectural detail, interesting though it is, does nothing to convey the welcome offered by the oldest inhabited manor house in the county. The splendid porch dates from 1282 with additions and alterations to the house undertaken in the fifteenth, seventeenth and twentieth centuries; the result is a home in the best English tradition.

Wilton House, Salisbury (plate 18)

A magnificent mansion, originally the site of an old-established abbey. The first private house was built here from 1542, traditionally to designs of Holbein the painter. Great damage was caused by a fire in 1647, and Inigo Jones was called in to rebuild the house, which he completed in 1653. A Lord Pembroke of the day designed and built the beautiful Palladian Bridge over the river Nadder in 1737. Very considerable alterations, inside and out, were made by James Wyatt from 1801, much of it in Gothic style. The Double Cube Room, unaltered since being designed by Inigo Jones and completed by his nephew after his death, is one of the most famous rooms in Britain. The house is filled with works of art and other treasures collected over the centuries.

WALES

Cardiff Castle, Cardiff

Although the site of a castle for 1900 years, it is the astonishing nineteenth-century interior created by William Burges with his patron the third Marquess of Bute which makes this one of the most visually exciting castles in Britain. Both men were dedicated medievalists and set up special workshops to produce the necessary carving, marquetry and murals which fill every corner. The fine roof garden with its mosaics and fountain is open only in summer.

Castell Coch, Tongwynlais, South Glamorgan

This fantasy castle, created between 1875 and 1890 from medieval ruins by William Burges for the Marquess of Bute, is set in a spectacular position overlooking the Taff Valley. This tiny castle was never intended to be lived in and Burges was able to give free reign to his exotic imagination in the interior decoration.

Chirk Castle, near Wrexham, Clwyd (NT)

This was built in 1310 at the same time as the castles at Conway, Harlech and Caernarvon. Chirk retains its unaltered medieval exterior, but successive generations have improved and decorated the interior which contains fine furniture and tapestries: the main reception rooms were lavishly decorated in the 1770s.

Erddig, near Wrexham, Clwyd (NT)*

Probably the only stately home where the visitor arrives in the estate yard and spends as much time below stairs as above. One of the most important and complete estates ever to have been given to the National Trust, a day should be allowed to do justice to the extensive displays illustrating how a self-dependent community was run. The interior contains many of the items listed in the inventory of 1726 as well as the accumulations of every generation since.

Penrhyn Castle, Bangor, Gwynedd (NT)

This enormous Norman-style castle with its massive surrounding wall and entrance lodges gave vital employment to many local workers between 1827 and 1840. Built by a slate baron, he had this unlikely and difficult material used for the immense Grand Staircase and for two bedsteads.

Plas Newydd, Llangollen, Clwyd (plate 22)

A striking black and white house bought in 1779 by the runaway Irish blue-stockings who became known as the Ladies of Llangollen. It is embellished inside and out with the extraordinary gifts and carvings brought by their many famous visitors.

Powis Castle, Welshpool, Powys (NT)*

Built of red limestone, and known in Welsh as the 'Red Castle', Powis stands dramatically on a height above its renowned eighteenth-century gardens. This strategic position on the Welsh border has had a fortification since the twelfth century but the present building dates mainly from the early seventeenth. The much altered interior contains tapestries, good furniture, fine plasterwork (1592), murals (1705) and a museum of items connected with Clive of India, whose family home it was.

SCOTLAND

Abbotsford House, Melrose, Roxburghshire (plate 26)

Nineteenth-century house overlooking the river Tweed, transformed by Sir Walter Scott at great (and keenly felt) expense into his personal museum of Scottish antiquities. Much of the house, and particularly the library, remains as it was at his death in 1832.

Blair Castle, Blair Atholl, Perthshire

Although this romantic castle dates back to 1269, it was Georgianised in the mid eighteenth century and the contents are by the leading craftsmen of that day. A splendid collection of Sèvres porcelain and three 'Treasure Rooms'. Among the displays here are miniature toys, and children's games belonging to successive Dukes of Atholl whose home it was.

Bowhill, Selkirk

The uncompromisingly plain nineteenth-century exterior houses an outstanding collection of pictures and furniture. Of special interest is the room devoted to relics and paintings connected with the Duke of Monmouth and Buccleuch and the study, with its portrait and mementoes of Sir Walter Scott, a near neighbour and friend of the family.

Braemar Castle, Braemar, Aberdeenshire

Built in 1628 as one of a chain of strongholds down the Dee. Although the interior was rebuilt for domestic use in 1748, the castle retains the evidence of its military past with the Laird's Pit for prisoners and the yett (defensive iron gate unique to Scotland), quite apart from its impregnable exterior.

Brodick Castle, Isle of Arran (NTS)*

Massive castle on the Isle of Arran defending the Firth of Clyde. Built originally in the fourteenth century, it was much enlarged in the seventeenth and nineteenth centuries and contains fine silver and pictures belonging to the Duke of Hamilton.

Castle Fraser, Sauchen (NTS)

Unchanged since its completion in 1636, the towers and turrets, the splendid frontispiece and the cable mouldings combine to make this one of the most appealing of the castles of Mar. A lucid exhibition in the courtyard explains the development of these castles and should be the first stop for visitors to the area.

Craigievar Castle, Aberdeenshire (NTS)

An unaltered example of the finest period of Scottish castle architecture, dating from the 1620s. The massive walls are topped with a splendid skyline of turrets, gables and cupolas.

Crathes Castle, Banchory, Kincardineshire (NTS)*

Arguably the best preserved sixteenth-century castle, inside and out, in Scotland. The remarkable painted ceilings, dating from 1599, owe their survival to having been covered with plaster; they remained unsuspected until 1876.

Culross Palace, Fife

This palace (simply the Scots term for a domestic house as opposed to a fortified one) was built between 1597 and 1611. It contains very fine examples of the painted panelled rooms which developed in Scotland due to the lack of native hardwood.

Culzean Castle, Mavbole, Ayrshire (NTS)*

The dramatic position on top of a sheer cliff overlooking the Firth of Clyde adds stature to this immense castle designed by Robert Adam in the 1780s. In addition to the building and decoration, much of the furniture and fittings was Adam's work; the Round Drawing room and the central oval staircase must rank as some of his finest and most imaginative designs.

Doune Castle, Doune, Perthshire

Once a royal palace for the Kings of Scotland, this impressive fourteenth-century castle was carefully and extensively restored in 1883. Sir Walter Scott in *Waverley* has his hero imprisoned here.

Edinburgh Castle

On one of the most romantic sites in the world, Edinburgh Castle has a lineage going back to legendary times. English and Scottish history has flowed through every room and courtyard. The rooms of the Old Palace (fifteenth-century) contain an enormous range of military and historical relics as well as the Honours of Scotland (the Scottish Crown Jewels), and the Armoury. There is a fine painted wooden ceiling in Queen Mary's Apartments where she gave birth to James, the king who was to unite the crowns of England and Scotland.

Glamis Castle, Glamis, Angus

An enormous combination of castle and palace filled with royal associations and legends. Built in the grey-pink local stone, it was remodelled in the seventeenth century on foundations of the eleventh century, when it was a hunting lodge for the kings of Scotland. The interior contains splendid plaster ceilings, carved mantelpieces and a notable panelled chapel with painted ceiling.

The Hill House, Helensburgh (NTS)

The house, furniture, fittings and colour schemes were designed by Glasgow architect Charles Rennie Mackintosh in 1902. It is a remarkable memorial to an artist many years ahead of his time.

Hopetoun House, South Queensferry, West Lothian

One of the largest and finest houses in Britain, standing on the Firth of Forth, and with contents to match the splendid architecture. Although another architect began the building in 1639, William Adam and later his sons Robert and John were responsible for the house as one sees it today. The paintings by, among others, Rubens, Titian, Teniers and Gainsborough, are a major attraction in a house which is rightly regarded as one of Scotland's chief glories.

Inveraray Castle, Argyll

An approach to the eighteenth-century headquarters of the Clan Campbell by water, with the Castle's piper playing on the quayside, epitomises the romance of the Highlands. The forbidding grey slate Gothic revival exterior hides a sumptuously decorated series of Georgian rooms; several of them are the work of John Adam, Robert's brother. A remarkable and decoratively arranged collection of muskets, Highland broadswords and Lochaber axes used by the Argyll militia in the Forty-five rebellion is on the walls of the Armoury Hall.

Kellie Castle, Fife (NTS)

Large seventeenth-century castle based on one built some three hundred years earlier. Recently restored, it contains good plasterwork and particularly attractive painted panelling dating, like that in neighbouring Culross Palace, from the first quarter of the seventeenth century.

Lauriston Castle, Edinburgh

An impressive house enlarged and built in this century on the remains of a sixteenth-century castle. Owned by the Corporation of Edinburgh and maintained as it was in about 1920. Contains among other things a good and unexpected collection of Derbyshire 'Blue John'.

Manderston, Duns

Completed in 1905, Manderston represents the epitome of Edwardian extravagance and ostentation and is seen today apparently untouched by subsequent fashions. The many rooms on three floors shown to visitors give a very authentic picture of the period. The charming marble dairy tucked away in the gardens should not be missed.

Mellerstain, Gordon, Berwickshire *

A vast mansion with superb views, designed by William Adam in 1725 and completed by his son Robert forty years later. The interiors by Robert are outstanding and contain much fine furniture.

Palace of Holyrood House, Edinburgh

The most important palace in Scotland and the residence of the Royal Family when visiting Edinburgh. The building was started in 1500, and considerable alterations were done in the seventeenth century. Magnificent collections of royal belongings.

Traquair House, Innerleithen, Peebles-shire

This mansion house, though considerably rebuilt in the seventeenth century, claims to be the oldest inhabited house in Scotland. It offers both history and treasures covering ten centuries. As an added attraction it is licensed to sell its own Traquair Ale, made in the two hundred-year-old Brew House.

FURTHER READING

Girouard, Mark. *Life in the English Country House*. Yale, 1978.

Girouard, Mark. *The Victorian Country House*. Yale, 1980.

Hill, Oliver, and Cornforth, John. *English Country Houses: Caroline 1625-1685*. Antique Collectors' Club.

Hussey, Christopher. *Georgian Houses* (three volumes). Antique Collectors' Club, 1987 (paperback).

Milne, James Lees. *English Country Houses: Baroque 1685-1715*. Antique Collectors' Club.

Nicolson, Adam. *The National Trust Book of Great Houses of Britain*. Weidenfeld, 1978.

Pevsner, Nikolaus. *The Buildings of England* series. Viking Penguin, various dates.

Waterson, Merlin. *The Servants' Hall*. Routledge, 1980.

Houses described in the gazetteer: Scotland and northern England.

91

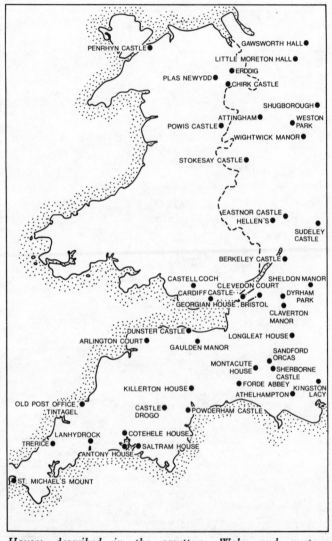

Houses described in the gazetteer: Wales and western England.

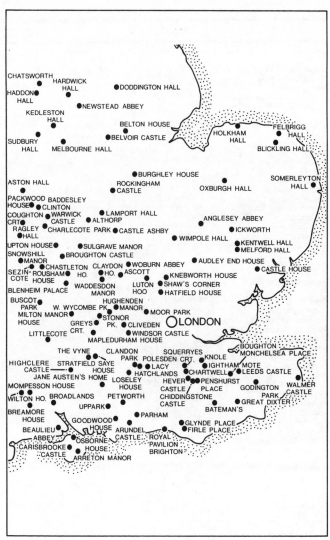

Houses described in the gazetteer: southern and eastern England.

INDEX